A LIFE
OF
DIVINE VICTORIES

an incredible journey in the arms of God

Modupe Josephine Fasusi

WESTBOW
PRESS®
A DIVISION OF THOMAS NELSON
& ZONDERVAN

WestBow Press books may be ordered through booksellers or by contacting:

WestBow Press
A Division of Thomas Nelson & Zondervan
1663 Liberty Drive
Bloomington, IN 47403
www.westbowpress.com
1 (866) 928-1240

ISBN: 978-1-4497-4481-6 (sc)
ISBN: 978-1-4497-5906-3 (e)

Library of Congress Control Number: 2012905540

Print information available on the last page.

WestBow Press rev. date: 06/24/2016

'The praying hand is the way
to Divine victories'

CONTENTS

THE DIVINE MISSION

"He who dwells in the secret place of the Most High, shall abide under the shadow of the Almighty. I will say of the Lord, 'He is my refuge and my fortress; My God in Him I will trust'. Surely He shall deliver you from the snare of the fowler and from the perilous pestilence; He shall cover you with His feathers; and under His wings you shall take refuge. His truth shall be your shield and buckler. You shall not be afraid of the terror by night, nor of the arrow that flies by day, nor of the pestilence that walks in darkness, nor of the destruction that lay waste at noonday. A thousand may fall at your side, and ten thousand at your right hand; but it shall not come near you. Only with your eyes shall you look, and see the reward of the wicked. Because you have made the Lord who is my refuge, even the Most High your dwelling place; No evil shall befall you, nor shall any plague come near your dwelling; For He shall give His angels charge of you, to keep you in all your ways. In their hands they shall bear you up; lest you dash your foot against a stone. You shall tread upon the lion and the cobra, the young lion and the serpent you shall trample under foot. Because he has set his love upon Me, therefore I will deliver him; I will set him on high, because he has known My name. He shall call upon Me and I will answer him; I will be with him in trouble; I will deliver him; with long life I will satisfy him, and show him My salvation." (Psalm 91:1-16)

Sometime in 2007 and later on April 14, 2011, I had the inspiration to write my experiences in books to honor God Almighty, for taking me through unforgettable life changing experiences between 1970 and 2010. The journey of course started many years earlier when I was born in Lagos Nigeria, but the peculiarities intensified about forty-two years ago. I was in bondage, my life was being manipulated by sorcerers and witches; I felt it, but didn't know what it was or what was happening to me. I couldn't describe the problems to people because they wouldn't understand or believe me; even I did not know what was happening to and around me at first, let alone articulate this intelligently to others. So I turned to God and sought answers and His deliverance; I had no other option. *Jeremiah 29:13 "And you will seek Me and find Me, when you search for Me with all your heart."*

The purposes of these writings are mainly to honor and glorify God, to show He lives—the same yesterday, today and tomorrow, to share with many others who are experiencing life's challenges, to strengthen others who are in transition from one season of life to another, to offer support to others seeking answers to whatever is happening in their lives right now, to encourage many others out of lethargy, to lead people to God, to guide others in bondage towards deliverance and freedom, and to confirm that prayer to God truly and really works.

The urgency to write remained an undying force even while I was running a Management & Business Consulting practice from 2001 to 2008. I tried to write several times about Human Resources consulting experiences; I even started in 2007 but didn't complete the book until 2008 when I relocated. Then something told me to write about my bizarre experiences for the world to read and for people to learn from these experiences, but put it off again and again. I was busy trying to gain full time employment or independent Consulting. At other times, certain unusual developments aborted these efforts I had made at full employment while in the US, from 2008 to 2011. In spite of the economic depression and all these challenges, the Lord said He had given me employment. I was looking in the wrong places, the job I was to do had already been given to me—the book project. Throughout these experiences described above, the Holy Spirit reminded me from time to time, of the book project I was assigned to do while doing some temporary or part time work.

So, by the middle of October 2010, allowing the will of God, I started to seek divine guidance as to what to write, how to write, what to focus on in the book, and other preparations needed for the project. By early December 2011, I started to put down ideas and thoughts about the book project. In the middle of December 2011, I started the draft of the first of what I hope will be many books in the series, As soon as I started, I couldn't stop; the information just poured out of my head until I completed the book at the end of February 2012.

I know you will enjoy the experiences I will describe, the hope they will inspire, and the strength they will encourage in you.

INTRODUCTION TO THE BOOK

This book titled 'A Life of Divine Victories . . . *an incredible journey in the arms of God*' is written as simple narrations of spiritual experiences and journey of about forty-two years, of an ordinary professional woman to all others who might be facing life's challenges, who may not be able to discuss in any meaningful way with others around, because they do not understand the issues experienced by that individual. As the problems increased and compounded, I was sure God was punishing me for my many sins and so I prayed more, fasted more, did more penance and resolved to seek more righteousness in all aspects of my life. This change worked for me, strengthened my faith, and took me in the direction of my destiny. As with most people in my generation, I grew up with the idea of 'God of punishment' more than anything else. Later on I understood that God is more compassion, loving, forgiving, and wholesome. I do not write as a scientific, extensive research based material for teaching. I am not a trained Pastor or teacher wishing to impact learning as in a class. There are many excellent scholastic literatures in the market place which fulfill that role. I only wish to share my learning from real life experiences with others. I hope to bring something different to readers in the series of writings. I will discuss and share unique personal spiritual experiences with readers in this incredible journey I went through in the arms of God, using the following outline-

- Sharing Experiences
- Awesome God
- Seeking God
- Jesus Christ, Divine Son
- The Holy Spirit
- The Blessed Virgin Mary
- Living in the Spirit
- Divine Communications

DEDICATION

This book is dedicated to Jehovah El Shaddai;

The "I am that I am";

The One, Eternal, and Almighty God

FORWARD

I was born as the last of a family of five children, four boys and one girl, me; the first of the boys died in childhood so we never really got to know him, leaving four of us. I was a late child and a pleasant surprise to my parents. We were a middle class family, with educated professional parents. My father was a church organist, teacher and later an Attorney for several years; while my mother was an active member of the church and a Social Welfare Officer working extensive hours to support families and children from challenging homes. So that we might understand our heritage fully, my father wrote his autobiography and gave each of us a copy. In that document, he reiterated the family's commitment to the Almighty God and the Catholic faith. This family heritage makes my brothers and I, fifth generation Catholics, and anointed instruments for God's purposes on earth. By God's holy anointing, all of us descendants of these families are not candidates for any satanic cult, sorcery and witchcraft. My brothers and I were raised as Catholic children, innocent and shielded from the world of evil, witchcraft, demonic realities, and activities, often spoken in whispers not to the ears of children. Sooner or later, unprepared Christian children would meet children of witches in schools, in churches or at work. It is better to open up the discussion, educate children early, and arm them with divine Godly Biblical weapons, before they go into the world.

I studied Psychology, and hold a bachelor's degree in that subject. I also hold the Master of Business Administration MBA. In the Clinical Psychology class, I learned about Psychological and Psychosomatic illnesses of varying degrees. I have also studied, worked, lived, and travelled between Africa, Europe, and the United States (US). Most Western treatments for psycho-pathology has focused consistently on the physiological, critical aspects of the sociological, but hardly recognizes the important aspects of the spiritual. If man exists in the body, spirit and soul, it then follows that any treatment of human psychological pathologies, must address his physical body, his mental health and his spiritual health. Ironically modern science had discovered the effect of the 'mind over matter', but the linkages between both, had so far not been fully adopted by scientists. The effects of the soul as an influencer over the mind had been largely ignored in the treatment or management of the psychopathologies of the mind, which reflect themselves in the life, behavior or physical health of the person. This contrasts the Eastern and the Developing worlds' alternative approaches, which use vocalized prayers to the patient, and herbal remedies for the body, while treating him at home or/and within the community. The ancient Chinese healing practices, the Native American, and the Native Mexican healing practices, all recognize and focus on the spirit, soul, and body, using both herbal and prayerful incantations in their healing practices. These methodologies use these comprehensive therapies and the spiritual prayer rituals on the 'being' (or spirit) of the patient because they understood the inseparability of the body, soul, and spirit. I refer to the ground-breaking Mental Health researches of Professor Thomas Adeoye Lambo,OBE. (1923-2004). He was the eminent scholar and Neuro-Psychiatrist from Abeokuta Nigeria, and also formerly the Deputy Director General of the W.H.O. (1973-1988). He was one of those who first proposed and adopted the practice of Home/Community based management of mental illnesses. It is in such an environment that prayers or prayerful incantations are usually applied during the treatment of the patient, with significant degree of successes.

The consequence of the limited approaches is that mental health problems become compounded, and often elude conclusive resolution, management, and treatment. According to various popular literatures on mental and behavioral sciences, they record a steady rise in cases of socio-pathology and psychopathology. In addition to physiological causes, substances abuses and environmental factors were listed as the usual culprits. What is more, new types of pathologies are being discovered or labeled periodically.

The World Health Organization W.H.O's Mental Health Atlas 2011 summarized findings from a global research on the subject as follows:

- Resources to treat and prevent Mental Health Disorders remain insufficient.
- Resources for Mental Health are inequitably distributed.
- Resources for Mental Health are inefficiently utilized.
- Institutional care for Mental Health disorders may be slowly decreasing worldwide.

The research also showed that there is a substantial gap between the burden caused by mental health disorders, and the resources available to prevent and treat them. It is estimated that four out of five people with serious mental disorders living in low and middle income countries do not receive mental health services that they need. The mission of the W.H.O in the area of mental health is to reduce the burden of mental disorders and to promote the mental health of the population worldwide. However, this responsibility cannot be fulfilled satisfactorily if countries lack basic information about the existing infrastructure and resources available for mental health care. The report further stated these findings:

Neuropsychiatric disorders are estimated to contribute to 13% of the global burden of disease. Though the extent of the burden varies from country to country, neuropsychiatric disorders account for a substantial amount of the disease burden in every country of the world. Moreover, results from previous editions of the W.H.O. Atlas suggest that the gap between burden and resources is large.

Mental hospitals are present in 80% of countries. Countries where mental hospitals do not exist include small islands in the Americas and the Western Pacific region, ten African countries, and some European countries with exclusively community-based systems of care, such as Iceland, Italy and Sweden. Globally, the median rate of mental hospitals is 0.03 per 100,000 populations. Similarly, there is significant regional variability in the rate of beds in mental hospitals; globally, there are 7.04 beds per 100,000 populations.

According to a recent article by the US, National Institute of Mental Health, NIMH, Mental disorders are common in the United States and internationally. An estimated 26.2 percent of Americans ages 18 and older or about one in four adults suffer from a diagnosable mental disorder in a given year. When applied to the 2004 U.S. Census residential population estimate for ages 18 and older, this figure translates to 57.7 million people.

Even though mental disorders are widespread in the population, the main burden of illness is concentrated in a much smaller proportion about 6 percent, or 1 in 17 who suffer from a serious mental illness. In addition, mental disorders are the leading cause of disability in the U.S. and Canada for ages 15-44. Many people suffer from more than one mental disorder at a given time. Nearly half (45 percent) of those with any mental disorder meet criteria for two or more disorders, with severity strongly related to comorbidity.

In the U.S., mental disorders are diagnosed based on the *Diagnostic and Statistical Manual of Mental Disorders, fourth edition (DSM-IV).*

Mood disorders include major depressive disorder, dysthymic disorder, and bipolar disorder.

- Approximately 20.9 million American adults, or about 9.5 percent of the U.S. population age 18 and older in a given year, have a mood disorder.
- The median age of onset for mood disorders is 30 years.
- Depressive disorders often co-occur with anxiety disorders and substance abuse.

Suicide

- In 2004, 32,439 (approximately 11 per 100,000) people died by suicide in the U.S.7
- More than 90 percent of people who kill themselves have a diagnosable mental disorder, most commonly a depressive disorder or a substance abuse disorder.
- The highest suicide rates in the U.S. are found in white men over age 85.
- Four times as many men as women die by suicide; however, women attempt suicide two to three times as often as men.

Schizophrenia

- Approximately 2.4 million American adults, or about 1.1 percent of the population age 18 and older in a given year, have schizophrenia.
- Schizophrenia affects men and women with equal frequency.
- Schizophrenia often first appears in men in their late teens or early twenties. In contrast, women are generally affected in their twenties or early thirties.

Anxiety Disorders

Anxiety disorders include panic disorder, obsessive-compulsive disorder, post-traumatic stress disorder, generalized anxiety disorder, and phobias (social phobia, agoraphobia, and specific phobia).

- Approximately 40 million American adults ages 18 and older, or about 18.1 percent of people in this age group in a given year, have an anxiety disorder.
- Anxiety disorders frequently co-occur with depressive disorders or substance abuse.
- Most people with one anxiety disorder also have another anxiety disorder. Nearly three-quarters of those with an anxiety disorder will have their first episode by age 21.5.

Panic Disorders

- Approximately 6 million American adults ages 18 and older, or about 2.7 percent of people in this age group in a given year, have panic disorder.
- Panic disorder typically develops in early adulthood (median age of onset is 24), but the age of onset extends throughout adulthood.
- About one in three people with panic disorder develops agoraphobia, a condition in which the individual becomes afraid of being in any place or situation where escape might be difficult or help unavailable in the event of a panic attack.

Obsessive Compulsive Disorder OCD

- Approximately 2.2 million American adults age 18 and older, or about 1.0 percent of people in this age group in a given year, have OCD.
- The first symptoms of OCD often begin during childhood or adolescence, however, the median age of onset is 19.

Generalized Anxiety Disorders GAD

- Approximately 6.8 million American adults or about 3.1 percent of people age 18 and over, have GAD in a given year.
- GAD can begin across the life cycle, though the median age of onset is 31 years old.

Social Phobias

- Approximately 15 million American adults age 18 and over, or about 6.8 percent of people in this age group in a given year, have social phobia.
- Social phobia begins in childhood or adolescence, typically around 13 years of age.

For the purpose of this book, our adoption excludes cases of Post-Traumatic Stress Disorder PTSD, Eating Disorders, Attention Deficit Hyperactivity Disorders ADHD, Autism and Alzheimer's disease. (Source: National Institute of Mental Health)

None of the above research, methodologies, and reports, involved or considered the spiritual aspect of human mental health, in the management, resources utilization or the professional human resources needed. It is about time to think outside the box, and consider inclusive methods of managing mental health. We have nothing to lose, but a lot to gain.

The normal or abnormal behavior of man must be studied, understood, appreciated, and managed through the three dimensions of the physical, mental, and spiritual: the body, the spirit (emotions), and the soul.

Unfortunately, many people today who suffer from demonic afflictions are considered to be mentally unbalanced or suffering psychological illnesses, or of anti-social behavior tendencies, or suffering one physical psychosis or the other. Unfortunately, only the sufferer goes through his horrific experiences which ultimately affect behavior and which often changes his life and orientation. It is only these end products that others around him see. Often these others are also ignorant as to how to help the infirmed/ afflicted spiritually. I have heard some doctors quick to categorize or classify strange, unexplained behaviors as psycho pathology. The point here is that such restrictive categorization may be destructive. This same concept of demonic afflictions has profound implications for human resources management, and other professionals who are involved in human behavior and activities.

On the other hand, Spiritualists, Priests, Pastors, Naturalists, and other gifted individuals, have not been able to collaborate with medical professionals for various reasons; they should now get together in cooperation with the medical professionals in the management of Psychopathologies. It has taken several decades for Law Enforcement Agencies to accept the help offered through Extra Sensory Perception ESP, in the enforcement of the law and in the prosecution of criminals. In addition, there are whole aspects of human physiology, human psychology and human mentality, which are impacted by the supernatural. Unfortunately science as an investigative methodology has not offered much help in exploring, understanding, and managing the spiritual dimension of man. This scope belongs to the Divine and the professionals who work in that sphere. It may be short sighted and unproductive to continue to deny the impact of the spiritual, in human behavior and existence, just because we do not understand it, or because we cannot dissect or control it. I know many wise professionals including medical doctors, who believe in divine healing of the body, soul, and mind. The positive holy spirits and indeed the evil demonic spirits, have the potential to influence the spirit of the person. The ramifications of this subject of demonic afflictions, and their effects on health, on child development, on behavior, and on society, are both complex and extensive, posing interesting possibilities for urgent research studies for all these professions I mentioned above. On January 17, 2012 at 1.30p.m.to 2.00p.m., I was lucky to tune in to a program by Sid Roth 'Its Supernatural', when Sid was interviewing Rebecca Greenwood and her mission on Freedom from demonic afflictions. The insufficiency of established systems, structures and methodologies at solving demonic problems, has led to the Lord bringing up anointed individuals, many of whom are in various churches, to do God's work. Elsewhere, I discussed this idea further under 'Who will I send'. Their discussion on that program was very instructive, about the subject of demonic afflictions of adults and children, in this day and age.

All of the experiences I will relate here are real life and true. However, I have disguised the name of the main woman who oppressed me for forty-two years. We live among evil forces, demonic powers, and principalities, just as the Bible had warned us. As the world gets smaller with globalization, international travels, immigration, and emigration, the dangers posed by satanic/demonic globalized activities on the move, have become real for all nations. We all had better take notice and examine our positions. Those of us, who don't have Extra Sensory Perception ESP, or spiritual insight, are unable to 'see' these entities with our five normal senses. Sometimes, even the proverbial sixth sense, is not enough; but that we are incapacitated by our limited senses does not mean that these forces do not exist. Some of my experiences actually seemed bizarre, but they were real. These writings should help us reassess how we view, manage and understand behavioral differences, abnormalities and pathologies. We must be slow, very slow to categorize individuals into our known mental abnormal groups and stereotypes.

December 2011.

⇥ CHAPTER 1 ⇤

SHARING EXPERIENCES

MAJOR VICTORIES

I had met a young student in school, sometime in the early nineteen seventies, during an inter school games event. I will call her Ms. ABCD for the purposes of this book. From the time I met her; she looked and behaved so helpless, weak, needing a friend and constant support, that I felt drawn to her apparent helplessness. She wanted to be school friends and so stuck very close to me and somehow all my previous friends from earlier schools gradually faded away from my life. Some unexplained quarrel would start a disagreement or some sudden hostility between us. Two of my close friends then queried me about my sudden friendship with this girl who came from a different background from ours, and innocently warned me to be careful. I explained that she had few friends at that time and that I felt she needed a friend in the new school. I accepted all as individuals whether poor, middle class or rich. During the holidays, I mentioned this girl to my mother who was familiar with and recalled her family history. She observed that it was strange that I would meet a grandchild of that family at school. She explained how her grandparents had worked for a prominent family, at a time when my mother was a niece and ward of the original mistress of the household. I didn't think of or recall this incident any more until a few years ago. Unfortunately, both of the girls mentioned above, died from car accidents several years after we had left school; one in 1976 while on the National service and the other sometime in the 1980s. May their souls rest in peace! Perhaps if I had listened and taken their advices, my life could have turned out differently. On the other hand, I know that

God charts and pilots our lives in such a way that we fulfill His purposes. It is also possible that I was meant to meet this entity, and through that encounter, for God to overcome her demonic spirit, so that a greater evil in the future may be averted.

I sat back some years ago to do a personal audit, review and assess my life's journey as I have done since 1980. It is to God's glory that I had made much progress in the lives I had touched positively, through the favor and blessings of God received, and the many spiritual steps taken. The list below also shows some of the different challenges I had experienced. There were many others which I am not yet able to discuss publicly even now. It was difficult to discuss these challenges with people I knew, at the time they occurred.

- Every month in 1970/1971, I began hemorrhaging blood and in terrible pain, different from usual menstrual cramps as if I was having miscarriages. These problems attracted my school Principal who advised me to see a doctor. Through the report we discovered there was no physical cause for these problems other than abnormal pre-menstrual syndrome (PMS); and still the problems persisted throughout the twenty-four months in school. I had to wear pads all the time. The Rev Mother and Principal then prayed with me and the problem stopped in my second year. I didn't realize that these attacks showed that demonic changes had been made in my body. I didn't even know that the divine victories had started even before this time. As a result of this experience, the Rev. Mother and I remained close even after I left the school and until her death some years ago. I gave her updates about my health, work, and life; and she continued to pray for me. I still cherish a small book gift from her titled 'The Precious Present'; this was supposed to help me through some of the difficult periods of my life, which I had shared with her.

- From the time I was in the university, like most young girls, I was concerned that my relationships with successive boyfriends were always brief and unproductive. I was embarrassed as I remained single and prayed about my situation. After some time, I mentioned this to my close friends and Ms. ABCD invited me to her white garment church, which I will call the Heavenly Church of Christ Worldwide (real name changed). I thanked her but turned her down as I explained that being a Catholic, I was not interested in changing to her church. I told her that in God's time, He would answer my prayers.

- Eventually, I got married at 28 years old, and within 1 month discovered that the man had a chronic mental health problem which the family had been managing carefully for several years, though concealed from me. The strange thing was that although we courted for one year, and interacted with friends, I didn't see this illness; all those around me who knew, held the information back for various reasons, prior to the wedding. It was as if I was blinded so that I would not see or know what I needed to see or know. The illness was sufficient grounds for annulment. I sought an annulment from the church and a divorce from the state. As a result of some problems, these took fourteen years, but I concluded the process successfully.

- Some years after, I again discussed this challenge with this Ms. ABCD who explained that many women had to do extra prayers to get what they wanted and invited me to join her church, again I turned her down explaining that while I didn't mind the prayers, but that I would not need to join her church to pray to God.

- A few years later and although I wanted children, and was healthy, I didn't get pregnant until I was 35 years old, and only after series of prayers of supplication. My doctors all confirmed I was healthy and in time, should bear children easily. I stepped up prayers and God answered my prayers, giving me a child whom I named Aduraseyi meaning 'The Result of Prayers'.

- One day, a male friend of mine woke up at his home with heavy bleeding scratch marks on his back. He had been attacked and scratched during his sleep the night before, and the marks were as if a lion or some huge cat had scratched the man's back.

The scratch marks were in locations where his hands could not reach. So he didn't scratch himself. Also his nails were not even long or sharp enough. We prayed over this strange phenomenon and washed the wound with holy water. We didn't know who was responsible for the strange attack, but learnt that this was a typical witchcraft attack.

- Ms. ABCD invited me to her church harvest ceremony at the Heavenly Church of Christ Worldwide somewhere on the outskirts of Lagos, some many years ago; I attended just to honor her and her partner. All invited guests who made some donations to the church's harvest were given parting gifts. I was presented with a bottle of 'sanctified' honey. We all stood at the alter area while the Church's Shepherd prayed. Ms. ABCD stood next to me as I held my gift in my two hands. Suddenly without any pushing or other force, the bottle 'flew' up and fell from my hands and broke with a loud noise on the church's floor, attracting the attention of the members and leader. Immediately, I knew without doubt that the bottle was moved from my hands by some strange force. I stood in shock and without a word, left the church. The leader, who had witnessed this very strange event, came down to sympathize and to replace the damage with some other gift. That minor incident was very revealing to the spiritual eye, and to all those present. After a few months Ms. ABCD informed me that the church leader died of some sudden illness.

- I had a strange illness between November 2004 and April 2005. I was installed the Regional President of an international professional association in October 2004 in the UK, and returned to Nigeria in November, only to fall ill. I progressively lost weight and by April 2005, had lost one-third of my normal body weight. I was actually dying on my feet and no one could help me. The doctors in Lagos didn't see anything wrong with me although I was losing weight. My co-workers thought I was dieting, was anorexic or had some contagious disease. My body weight went from 172lbs., to 115lbs., having lost 57lbs., which was one-third of my weight in three months, November 2004

4

to January 2005. I looked like a walking skeleton and took a picture of myself. So I prayed like a warrior again, and the Lord God Almighty rescued me on April 26, 2005, right in my house. I had woken up on that fateful day, too weak to walk from the bedroom to the sitting room. As I sat down on the settee the Holy Spirit told me to go get my hymn book and to sing a song of Healing, titled *"A Powerful Healer is Present Here; Jesus the Consoler"*.

The picture was taken on February 16, 2005, three months into the unexplained illness when my body weight reduced to 115lbs, 2/3 of normal. I lost 1/3 of total body weight.

The message was clear and unmistakable. I sent my driver to get the hymn book for me from my bedroom; I was too weak to walk back into my bedroom. He got the book and *I started to sing the first sentence of the hymn, and within seconds, **I actually felt life rush back into my body, and I felt better and better right there. I felt new blood rushing through my veins and all over my body. So I sang the whole hymn and became stronger; suddenly in my body I knew I had been healed**.* So I called my brother, a doctor in the US and told him of the development that morning. He advised that I should still come over for the medical check-up earlier arranged so as to confirm what had happened. While in the US, I went through a battery of laboratory tests, medical examinations and diagnostics physicals for five weeks from May to July 2005. At the end of the period the specialist doctor concluded and told me that I was in great health. He did say that I seemed to have had a deadly bacteria which was difficult to discover except through a biopsy, and even also was very difficult to treat; and being so elusive was usually life threatening. He explained that food poisoning may cause the crises, but was surprised that I was healed completely. He wanted to know what medication I had taken before I came to see him. I told him that I had only taken my usual multi-vitamins, nothing more, but then told him of my divine experience and the healing power of God Almighty. Later, from books and public teachings, I understood that it is the practice of witches to drain blood from their prey, and that witches were draining my blood with a view to killing me. They failed because God held me in His arms, and on that fateful day, when my life was almost depleted, God stepped in and revived me.

- I recalled that I was invited to a wedding ceremony by Ms. ABCD. Somehow we were not fed at lunch at the wedding party that day although this was most unusual. After a while, we left by about 5p.m., and still rather hungry. She took me home in her car, and as we got to my house, she offered me an apple which she claimed was left in her basket in the car. I accepted and ate this apple. Perhaps the apple was poisoned, but I couldn't prove this. I stopped all outings with this woman from that time.

- These problems worried me a lot, since they were affecting me gradually both mentally, socially and physically. Again, I mentioned this at a prayer group meeting in my house and asked members to pray for me. Later this woman invited me to her church in order to help find solutions to the problems. By that time, I was sure someone was behind these destructive phenomena, but couldn't yet identify who. All the same I turned this woman's invitation down again.

- A neighbor had attended my birthday get-together, in 2001. He was one of the last guests to leave, and so spent some time talking to Ms. ABCD and her husband in the garden for a while. Soon after, this neighbor invited me to discuss some important matter. Thinking he had some family crises and needed help, I went along with one of my domestic staff as chaperon. This neighbor was reluctant to open discussions until I prompted him, since I was on my way to an outing that day. Suddenly and in his opening words, the neighbor simply started to curse me, without provocation, without any reason whatsoever. I stood shocked, rooted for a minute or so, then walked out with just a sentence. "That is not my portion". I reported this incident to a family member of the man and also to his wife after sometime. I know that '*A person blessed by God cannot be caused.*' It was later I learned through divine and prophetic revelations that demonic persons can take over the bodies, spirits and aura of other persons, in order to do havoc; for example, to deliver her curses. I understand also that it is possible for evil powers to enter into the spirit of others, to carry out destructive activities so that the real instigator would remain shielded and anonymous. In other words, they do evil by proxy. The Holy Spirit is truly amazing; and I am alive, well, and prospering today by the grace of God. He is a mighty God indeed and delivers those who call on Him.

- From the time I started to work in a firm in Lagos in 1976, I faced several administrative crises; this continued at every company where I had worked, until 2008 when I left finally for the United States. Lightening did strike over and over again in the same place. The repeated tragedies and series of problems were uncanny, and certainly unusual. At that time, I attributed the problems to company politics and jealousy. I was wrong.

- It was in 2006 or 2007 that God revealed to me what was going on, and delivered me totally from this curse, placed by demonic persons over me. The power of God is truly immense. We do not have to suffer demonic oppression of any kind, if we only take our problems to God. The blood of Jesus fights for us regularly.

- On March 4, 2008 at 11 a.m. just before I left for the United States, a woman called my phone and delivered curses to me through the phone. Unfortunately, an office staff was the one who took the call and heard the satanic message. She explained that the caller had first called my name before she delivered the curses. I blessed my staff immediately but returned all curses to the sender.

"The Lord is near to all who call upon Him; to all who call upon Him in truth." Psalm 145:18.

War of Tongues

Recently, in the personal review I referred to above, I listed the times and instances when someone close to me and therefore credible in the opinion of others, had started a destructive but false rumor or accusation against me. These are the ones I knew of and could recall so far. When these have happened in the past forty years, I would pray seriously and fasted for days, and suddenly the 'crises' would vanish, and somehow the truth would be revealed and I would be vindicated. This soon became the pattern of the affliction. During the crises however, a lot of damage would have been done. Sometimes I lost the chances of promotion or appointments or consulting businesses. Often I lost dignity, respect, honor, and goodwill. Why was I being so devastatingly attacked over and over again? Who was doing this?

For many years I saw the incidents as isolated, easily explained by other business or jealousy reasons. I truly didn't see them as a strategic whole. The fact that there was a pattern to the problem told me they were not accidental, but deliberate occurrences. Who was engineering such destructive acts? I didn't know. I complained to all the people who were close to me. Soon after, and as I moved closer and closer to God, He started to reveal secrets to me. I saw more and more, and understood situations better and better. The holy Bible called this the 'Spirit of Discernment'. I started to see these problems as a whole picture of a deliberate attempt to destroy my reputation, my good name and honor. It is the combined effects of these incidents that I concluded are enough to cause paranoia, or neurosis, but for the grace of God, who has sustained me. These harrowing experiences were truly devastating, but that was not my portion. Although the enemy had planned a nervous breakdown for me, God stopped and returned this evil back to senders. God had remained my strength and succor through all these trials. He had given me the courage to continue, and had kept me healthy and victorious.

1. 1971. I was staying in the home of my guardians while I attended a high school in a town outside Lagos, Nigeria; someone started a rumor that I was sleeping with a certain elderly man. At that time I was a virgin and was not sleeping with any man. I had to go to the daughter, a family friend to exonerate myself. I

wondered how this type of rumor started since there was no truth in it whatsoever; but soon dismissed it altogether.

2. 1972. There was another rumor, but I did not know the full story here. I only knew it was a nasty story, which I got to know of, when an old family friend looked at me one day, with undisguised hostility and snubbed me. I asked for further details, but he didn't want to discuss it any further.

3. 1975. A cousin who was living in my house started another rumor that I was responsible for her life's problems. This she claimed explained her lack of progress and my siblings' obvious progress. Of course there was no truth in this. Our parents were industrious and ambitious for us, encouraging us to aspire to great heights. Their words inspired us all and each of us had to struggle through some years of education and professional challenges to reach enviable levels of successes; every single one of us. Later on, the cousin and her senior sister wrote me a letter of apology over this matter. I was concerned but decided to forgive the cousin, forget it all and move on.

4. I discovered sometime later that the crises with lies and rumors, known as the 'War of Tongues,' resulted from Ms. ABCD dropping subtle, and later open lies to my family members, to other friends she met through me, and also business contacts. At other times she would enter into the bodies of others to cause damage. As usual none of those who heard, would verify the deadly lies with me, but believed. Initially, I never suspected who was behind the rumors, I however prayed for God's vindication, over and over again. This went on for several years.

5. 1984. In the year I was to be promoted in a manufacturing company where I worked, someone started a rumor and instigated an audit investigation into my department. I actually saw this first in a dream. I was falsely accused of sharp unethical practices in supervising a section of the department. An audit investigation was conducted, at the end of which I was exonerated, and commended for running a near perfect department. This

came after I had lost the promotion chances. I prayed and asked God to save me from this crisis. He showed me in a dream which of my seniors was behind this crises, and assured me He would save me. Many years later a colleague called me to warn me to be careful of Ms. ABCD. I understand that she had contacted my senior colleague to instigate the audit, but I didn't believe the caution and the implication. That colleague died a few years later of some strange illness. This was another indication I had, that some demonic spirit was working to destroy me. The above catalogue of events was difficult to explain to anyone, let alone convince others about a conspiracy theory which even I could not see at first, but for the grace of God, I saw later.

6. 1987/1988. I was living in an apartment on the Lagos Mainland; and my apartment was opposite that of one of the owner's children and her husband. Two cousins were also living with me at that time. Suddenly another rumor erupted that I was sleeping with a neighbor's husband. She was so furious she attacked me physically, and a fight erupted. I reported the matter to her parents, assured all I had no relationship with the man who actually worked and lived somewhere in the northern part of the country. He came home on few occasions and I hardly ever saw him. At that time we all thought that the lady (wife) was either hallucinating or someone was feeding her wrong information purposely to create a crisis; and wrote the matter off that way. The result was that I left that apartment soon after. This matter was widely spread in the church she and I were attending at the time, and I was again discredited for a while until her father completely exonerated me.

7. 1989/1999. I left the manufacturing firm, and joined a merchant bank for two years, then a commercial bank. After six years, and just when I was expecting to be promoted a serious crises arose and again an investigation ensued, concerning authorization for the employment of staff, and that the relevant approvals were not found in the files. After seven days of prayer and fasting, I found my copies of the said approvals which I didn't even remember I had kept. One day while resting at home, the Holy

Spirit led my steps to a pile of old papers in my study, where I found the critical papers, in a box of archived papers. In the meantime, I was humiliated and despised throughout the bank, by the time the truth was revealed, even those colleagues who were used to instigate the crises, came to apologize to me. My then supervisor affirmed privately later, that I was wronged and deserved to have been promoted. Of course it was too late by then. The bank became distressed soon after and I left for a Consulting firm.

8. 1997. Again a cousin, who had returned from the United Kingdom, had asked to live with me, until she could find her feet. My brother introduced her to her boyfriend when he came home on a visit. I had welcomed the family and entertained them extensively, and encouraged the relationship, as he was genuinely interested in her. The family invited us to a wedding by another member of their family. Instead of attending, I encouraged my cousin's mother to attend in my place. Suddenly and soon after the man stopped calling and broke off the relationship. He later confirmed to my brother that my niece had told him another deadly rumor about me. I was not even aware of this rumor until the story erupted. The man was so upset with her that he ended their relationship and observed that my cousin must be an ungrateful person, and he didn't want to continue their relationship any longer. I was stunned about this second campaign of calumny, of destruction from a family member.

9. In all my adult life, I was never aware that the church I normally attended acknowledged this sort of demonic affliction and problem, or had a solution for it. Sometime in 1997, while attending a Charismatic church, which had prayer warfare against unknown, forces afflicting members, I sought serious solutions to my spiritual problems. While there another rumor erupted from the Church leader whose romantic advances I had rejected, that I wanted a relationship with him but he declined. His then girlfriend started a huge war with me. It took a long time before she got to know the truth of the story. Eventually I had to drag my father and other former leaders of the church

with me to confront the leader, who denied starting the rumor or any wrongdoing. I left the church thereafter.

The fact that I saw the positive intervention of God after every one of these rumors confirmed to me that I was under a demonic hold or sorcery, and must intensify prayers.

10. 1998. I attended a Business School between 1996 and 1997. I did some part time work with the School until I found full time employment. Suddenly and without warning, another rumor started. I do not know the details of this rumor to date, but it went on for about fifteen years. This was so damaging and strategically offensive in all respects. Everyone I knew from that school distanced themselves from me immediately, my new clients who all had connections to the school, shut their doors against me and my business. After many days of prayers and fasting the event subsided. Later I learned that someone who had some connections to Ms. ABCD started the war and series of rumors, but that sometime in 2011, the truth also became revealed.

11. 2000. I survived these problems only through prayers and the protection of God; as I overcame one, another one would surface. A relation was told in prophetic revelation that certain individuals who would otherwise benefit from his Construction project were scheming to destroy the project and holding it down. I didn't know all these then except that the various members of the extended family began to treat me like a leper and traitor. I was despised by all, until I got the facts from one member who revealed what was happening. Apparently fingers were pointed at me as the culprit. I prayed and fasted for days, and asked God to reveal the truth. After a while and much suffering, the truth came directly to my relation. A prayer meeting revealed to him and other family members present, that I had a lot of trials and tribulations in my life, but that in spite of these, I would pray for all my family members, as well as for myself every time I prayed; but that I was innocent of the charges. Luckily for me, the truth

came out in the presence of another cousin, who subsequently revealed this to the rest of the family.

12. 2001-2003. I started to make relocation plans so that I could join all my brothers who were all United States citizens, having studied and settled there. I realized that I had to escape from my environment as soon as possible. There was nothing keeping me back except the renovation of my bungalow, my consulting business and the international organization I belonged to. Ms. ABCD tried to dissuade me from relocating, but I told her there was no going back on the relocation plan. I understood that she needed to continue to see me in the flesh, to feed on my aura, to continue to attack my spirit, and so as to carry out her deadly plots.

13. 2004/2006. I became the Regional President of an international association of women. In 2005 different kinds of conflicts erupted between some members and me. We managed to overcome these only through prayers. By 2006, just before I left office, several other rumors erupted. I soon became the topic of general discussions in town. These persisted until I relocated to the United States in 2008. Again I prayed and asked God to rise up again against the attacks. I then resigned from the Association following my relocation.

14. From about 2006/2008 someone began again to spread yet more deadly rumors, lies and deliberate slander about me. This was so widespread and so evil that all my neighbors, hairdressers, estate agents, association members, colleagues, business associates, clients, church members, and even some family members abandoned me, treating me like a leper. I wanted to know what was going on, but no one would tell me what was happening. Up till today, I only have an idea but never had any confirmation of what was being said, or who was saying these destructive things. So again and again, I prayed for God to overturn this problem. He did, gradually He rolled back the slander and returned me to His grace and peace.

15. 2007. Following from the above, different undisclosed rumors erupted at the Church I attended. Immediately, male and female members who were previously 'friends' of mine, actually openly shirked away from me, several Sundays when I went to Church. People would move away from the seat where I was, and I was often left alone on my seat. I was so desolate I took the matter to the Parish Priest who advised me to continue to pray, say the Holy Rosary and wait for God's intervention. The isolation and hostility continued and I stopped going to the church thereafter, and went to another. The stories soon followed me everywhere and people avoided me, but I never stopped praying for deliverance. In spite of these experiences, God said I was to remain in His presence always, and no matter what challenges I may face, and which were trying to prevent me being in His presence. So I asked Him to direct me to the church I would attend seeing as I was driven from churches by the devastating rumors. While searching for churches on the television and watching religious programs, he led me to Laughter Foundation Cathedral Church, Lagos. I remained determined to show myself before God regularly at prayers. Although the rumors followed me there, I remained unmoved, but showed up regularly before God.

16. 2007/2008. About this time, someone started a campaign of another set of rumors to destroy my firm. I had taken one of the staff to a meeting one day when I realized there was unease at the meeting, after a short break. Apparently, the client received a deadly communication from the staff I had taken to the meeting. Needless to say, I lost the client. A divine message had been sent to me earlier that year, where I was warned that one of my staff would become a satanic vessel, to bring destruction to the firm and so I led a prayer, in the office to avert this evil. She had failed because God sustained the firm which relocated with me to the United States.

17. 2008/2009. I also suffered three consecutive rumors at the church I attended here in the United States. An innocent incident where I had helped a man in tears out of a major personal family crisis,

became the subject of a devastating dirty rumor, until after much praying and fasting, God revealed the truth subsequently to the church members. The consequence was that the people who had treated me with kindness and respect ran away from me. Soon after, the truth came out and got to me. So I celebrated at a Thanksgiving at the church. Immediately after, two series of serious rumors erupted again, and I knew I was truly under demonic warfare, which I now know can follow the target everywhere. I only knew what was happening from the deadly antagonistic reactions from church members. I reported to the Parish Priest who assured me that I was probably mistaken when I reported the matter of this unrelenting oppression, and left that church soon after.

18. When I heard this I realized that all these problems were not normal, and indeed instigated by some form of sorcery or demonic influence. It was not natural to be so afflicted and persistently targeted with destructive stories, rumors and lies, even by strangers who did not know me enough to plan or plot evil; unless these strangers were demonic contacts or agents themselves. I understand that this is called the 'War of tongues', a terrible and devastating weapon used by witches against target opponents, in order to multiply adversaries. The multiplication of adversaries is aimed at creating stress and removing peace from the target person. I also understand that a particular demonic power, A—(full name withheld in this print), was the demon assigned to harass and constantly afflict me. Such affliction by demons usually leads to mental health problems for the person. All these revelations were strange to me, and very frightening. By now I realized I was in a deadly battle for survival. Although I was now living in the United States, the battle continued. I went into prayer warfare again and affirmed to the Father that I would not go under. I reminded Him of His covenant of protection to me. I boldly demanded that He faced my enemies and deliver me completely. I recalled for God, all the major damages which continued to be done to my good name and reputation. I cried to Him about how all these series of stories, destructive, and unceasing crises had started to affect

my business, and health. I knew I got God's attention fully that day. He answered me in a profound and amazing way; He said "Be still and know that I am God". Nothing more, nothing less. This was enough for me.

19. During my last visit to Lagos in 2009, when I attended a church service again, I heard the Pastor talk of a revelation about how a certain woman in the church, was going through serious demonic warfare, and about the warfare of dog attacks in dreams, over and over again; but that it was God Himself who was fighting these battles for this lady. He revealed that the dogs which were witches, also meant that the woman would not be married because a demonic woman had kept her single, imprisoned, and in bondage. The goal of this demonic woman he said was so that the woman in bondage would support the other woman financially, as if playing the role of a husband; but God said that the woman in bondage would overcome all obstacles because the chain was broken that day. I had no doubt he was referring to me. I stood shocked but thankful to God.

So I challenged God next and asked why He allowed me to be oppressed devastatingly and socially wherever I went and especially in the house of God. Nobody knew me long enough in the new church, and no one was jealous of me to want to cause me this level of damage.

On my return to the United States, the Holy Spirit directed my steps, and I went to Mother Mary at the church in N.W Washington D.C., mentioned elsewhere in this book. God's reply was that He would never give us experiences which we were unable to cope with, and that He is with me. That told me also that God saw these events and permitted them, for a positive divine reason. This new realization became somewhat reassuring.

In all these situations, I looked guilty although I was totally innocent. All those who heard the stories usually would not tell me what they heard, but judge me as guilty, and would avoid any contact with me. They would also not even bother to confirm whether the stories were true or not. They would choose to believe the worst, and would act on it, but have since found out that God is the only reliable friend to have and to hold. Again and again, God would deliver and vindicate me.

Witchcraft or demonic attacks lead to creating repeatedly negative or hostile external environment, which creates an intense negative emotion, stress and anxiety in the target person. When this is sustained for months and years, the result is that the spirit of the person comes under attack, leading to the loss of *peace.* It is this loss of inner spiritual peace which destroys the physical body and emotion of the person. The outward evidence of this loss situation is the abnormalities in body and behavior. When the person who is in this situation is unable to communicate effectively with others, receive support and understanding from them or if others isolate the person due to fear, then the problem becomes compounded. The solution to this situation is **Prayer.** This is why Jesus Christ gave and left all true Christians His peace, which passes all understanding, to sustain us through situations of life's challenges.

WARS OF ANTAGONISM

- My experience under what I classified as 'War of Antagonism' was equally bizarre. Gradually and sometimes suddenly people around me became very hostile and antagonistic. Simple issues became wars of hostilities. I faced hatred everywhere. I was in perpetual conflicts with everyone around me. I experienced unexpected and sudden opposition and antagonism from acquaintances. It took me twelve years to complete some simple renovation of my five—bedroom bungalow. Every contractor, every maintenance worker, and every employee who worked for me ended up leaving as a result of some confusion, disagreement, one conflict or another. I was especially careful with neighbors and acquaintances. I made extra special efforts at harmony with all. At first I thought I needed to change my behavior because I too might be responsible for the way others around me reacted to me. So I did some introspection and began a deliberate effort at peaceful co-existence with others. I became even more polite, friendlier, more humble, more accommodating of others faults, and more tolerant of contractors.

- Then one day while speaking to a sympathetic Christian cousin, she hinted that I might be suffering from what is known as the 'Mark of hatred', usually placed on the forehead of victims unknowingly. Immediately, I recalled my mother warning me several years previously when I was a young girl, never to allow anyone, stranger or known persons to touch my head under any guise; that such people would pretend that there was some strange object on your head and that they wanted to remove it for you. She warned that this was the usual guise to touch and mark the person, on the forehead. Immediately, I also recalled that on one occasion, Ms. ABCD had in fact used the ruse to touch my head at a time I was totally trustful. I also recalled that although I had resisted initially, somehow, I found myself conceding my head to her. That was when I was marked.

- Several months later, this mark was removed from my head during a church service on January 27, 2008. The church Pastor had said in a word of prophecy, that "a certain lady in this service had been marked on her forehead, the skin there is darker than the rest of her skin; and that God had just removed this mark forever." I knew my prayers were answered and that he was referring to me.

- Knowing what I had just experienced, I prayed again for God to help me complete the renovation of my house so that I could complete and execute my relocation plans, without further delays. Amazing grace, after the series of prayers and fasting, I was told in my spirit, (I believe the Holy Spirit put a suggestion in my mind), to go to three churches to perform some cleaning assignment in the churches; and that as I did so, I should ask God to clean my house of all hindrances, demonic objects and mountains of delay. If I told anyone, they would not believe me, and so did not. So without question, I went to three churches as directed and did as I was told to do very early about 5a.m. each day to carry out my cleaning mission. Amazing God, thereafter. I was able to complete the renovation without further troubles. It worked like magic. Truly there are many things stranger than fiction in this world we live in. We had better hold fast unto God to take us through, because we can never do so on our own strength since we constantly wrestle against principalities and evil spirits in high places.

As a result and for many years I was severely disoriented and confused, even though I did all the normal routine of work, socials, and professional activities. I often walked about like a zombie, pondering all the bizarre happenings around me. I remained in this state of prolonged shock for years. The only thing which made sense was my daily prayer moments. Everything else was unreal. Except for God, I was completely alone. My brothers and all other members of my larger family were in the United States or some other distant places. It was in this state that one friend or another, one distant relation or another, departed or separated from me, no matter how much I tried to hold onto them emotionally, as I sought their support in the state I was. Those were emotionally stressful periods, but God walked me through, encouraged me, strengthened me and kept me together. Everyone who dug a pit for me fell into the pit themselves. The grace of God had returned the evil back to the enemies and senders.

So in all of the above situations which I described earlier the effects on me were as follows:

- They isolated me from society and social contacts.
- They destroyed my good name and reputation, for a short while.
- They isolated me from my family members who believed I was guilty as accused.
- They destroyed my business also for a while.
- Initially some people thought I was imagining all these and was probably losing it, until the stories hit them.
- They caused me great discomfort, emotional trauma, humiliation, stress, anxiety, fear for my life and physical distress.

- It is easy to destroy the person who stands alone, they thought. However I was not alone; God stood strongly behind me, shielding me in His arms.

AMAZING DIVINE REVELATION

At first I didn't know who was behind these series of crises, and I complained out loud to all those around me; but by 2000 I realized Ms. ABCD was the evil and dangerous enemy. She had reported to me that her step-children had called her a witch at different times. At first I had hesitated and did not believe the accusation, but soon realized that the step-children could be right. That she brought this matter to me was a way for me to know what I needed to know. She might have been preempting me from hearing this story elsewhere, but the Holy Spirit was making it possible for me to know this secret through her own statement. I needed to hear with the spiritual ear. At first it was difficult to actually believe a person could be so devastatingly demonic; plotting and executing destruction against several people including me all her life. Over the years, I had encouraged and supported the professional development and investment progress of this woman, as I did for all those who were close to me. Furthermore I was reluctant to hold anyone responsible for my plight, since such an allegation was impossible to prove at first. So I was in denial and disbelief for about two years, and then went into shock for about one year after the truth was no longer deniable. I soon realized that she is what she said she is. Having introduced her to my family, I had inadvertently brought them into danger. I prayed to God to protect all of them. Thereafter I took definite steps to restrict contact with her.

Thereafter, I asked God to tell me what I needed to know quite plainly, so as to remove any remnant of doubt. **I had prayed and fasted for twen-one days or so, and asked God to tell me plainly who was attacking me, so that I know. I also asked Him to tell me what to do.**

On July 8, 2006, I had a dream in which *I had been climbing a ladder and was resting at a first landing; I gradually pulled Ms. ABCD onto the ledge where I was standing to rest for a while before climbing higher. Suddenly, she pushed me down from the ladder and I started to tumble down. Immediately I woke up.* Then I prayed because the implication of the dream and the culprit were clear.

Soon after, I stopped all residual interactions with this woman; I called her and asked her not to come near me again. Even then it wasn't the kind of matter you discussed with anyone. When I recalled all that I had been through, I knew she was going to fight a deadly battle, but I was assured that the power of God was mightier than whatever power she was using. God said I should leave her to Him, that He was going to make her an example for the world to see. God also said that her story and His powers would be recounted for generations. Every time, at every turn, the pit which the enemy dug for me became their portion-they fell into it; one by one, she and her group members. At this point I realized she was in consort with some group of other women around her. My parting sentence to her was 'Who is greater than Jehovah El Shaddai? There is no power greater than the power of God Almighty and the Holy Spirit reveals all secret things.'

In their arrogance, the enemies saw me as the opponent, an easy target; they were blinded to see the awesome power of God standing mightily behind me. The Lord God began, one by one to destroy all the witches and sorcerers around me. When the enemy planned death for me or my own, God cancelled such death over me and returned the death or the evil machinations to such individuals and their household.

Many people, who are experiencing bizarre situations in life, should know and understand that the deadly powers of evil exist all over the world. The sooner people understand this reality, the faster and easier they would find solutions to life's challenges. Our greater consolation is that whatever the enemy throws at us, the power of God is far greater. We must find a place under God's power immediately. *Isaiah 43:2 said "When you pass through the waters, I will be with you and through the waters; they shall not overflow you; when you walk through the fire, you shall not be burned, nor shall the flame scorch you."*

GOD'S MIGHTY HAND IN BATTLE

On March 15, 2008 and after a private prayer session, the word of God was delivered by a visiting sympathetic Pastor at my home. *"The God of Daniel in the lion's den; the God of Moses on the banks of the Red sea; and the God of David before the Goliath has risen against your enemies and had given you victory."* Apparently, I was imprisoned in the den of satanic lions and God delivered me. I was oppressed for about forty years, by witches with the power of pharaoh; but God delivered me from slavery and bondage. I was forced into battle with the mighty Goliath of witchcraft; and through the power of God, he was defeated.

That prophetic message was a confirmation that even before the pronouncement, God rose up against my enemies and took over the battles for me. He gave me His covenants of total protection in Psalm 91: 1-16, and to destroy all those who oppressed me, in *Isaiah 49: 25 & 26 "Even the captives of the mighty shall be taken away and the prey of the terrible shall be delivered; For I will contend with those that contend with thee and I will save thy children; And I will feed them that oppress you with their own flesh and they shall be drunken with their own blood as with sweet wine, and all flesh shall know that I the Lord I'm thy Savior and thy Redeemer, the Mighty One of Jacob."* These bible verses and divine promises have been fulfilled in my life ever since then, as I looked back at happenings around me. They did not know, but have found out the awesome and mighty power of God. To end the battles God sent the Holy Blessed Virgin Mother Mary to tell me in a dream what steps to take, and what to do. I did as she advised and was saved ever since. My Holy Blessed Mother in heaven was watching over me all the time.

Bishop Matthew Ashimolowo, of the Kingsway International Christian Center KICC in London, UK conducted and reported a ground breaking historical research some years ago; which revealed and identified certain aspects of the origins of demonic influences and powers in Africa, the West Indies, and in other places around the world. I sat glued to the television set, watched and listened to his teachings throughout the series of his lectures. In the United States, I have also seen, and read some books about how to survive demonic warfare; the nature of demonic warfare; and fighting against demonic attacks. In all these instances, the readers are advised to call on the blood of Jesus and the power of God Almighty. We cannot fight them in the flesh, but only in the spirit. That means our spirit must unite with the Divine Spirit, to enable the One and true God to fight the battle on our behalf. We approach the Father only through prayers, worship, adoration, listening for His directives in His replies, and obeying Him totally.

During sleep and just before I woke up on Saturday August 16, 2008, I had an amazing dream. I found myself wearing a white garment, and standing in a stream or river, washing some dirt, grime and mud off my body; and I walked out of the water looking around me in surprise and embarrassed about the wet clothes clinging to my wet body. Then a man who was standing near the banks of the river spoke out to me, he said "This is how God brings a person to wash in the river so as to make them clean. You must have three Thanksgiving to God in different churches, and at the event, you will prostrate seven times to God in each ceremony". I woke up and sat still fully understanding this dream. All the mud and dirt thrown over me have been washed away by God. I emerged clean, shining, vindicated and justified. This is the amazing power of God.

I have listed these experiences just for information and to let you have an idea of what Divine victories had occurred for me in the past forty-two years. I am sure there are several others I didn't even know about, because God had taken care of the matter. At first I was spiritually blind and when I first saw the events I did so as individual events but didn't view any of these matters in a consistent manner; but even the greatest skeptic would begin to wonder what was going on with me. I soon began to see a whole picture, a plot of persistent destruction from warfare of all sorts, including the "war of tongues." Why was I being so devastatingly attacked over and over again? And why was God allowing it. I needed the irritations to get closer to God; to seek Him more and more as my life, destiny and mission actually depended on it. No one else except God could have delivered me. I have heard some television preachers explained that the enemy fights you not only for today, but because of your tomorrow which they know you are destined for; others had also explained that God allows a person to go through this fire and irritation in order to turn the rough coal into diamond, an irritating pebble in an oyster, into a beautiful pearl, useful for the ultimate destiny designed by God. The Lord said He had waited ten years for me to hear Him, His warnings to me and His mission for me. I was so occupied with world activities, and getting nowhere, that I didn't quite listen or hear the voice of God. That was dumb. For this I suffered severely through years of bondage under witchcraft attacks and demonic intrigues, which engulfed and nearly drowned me. The grace, mercy, and power of God sustained me, and then vanquished all my enemies one after another. "Glory be to God in the Highest".

The Lord God of Israel instructed that I tell these stories so that the whole world would get to know that activities of demonic agents among us are real. I survived only because God saved me. He first reminded me of this instruction on January 3, 2009, then on November 29, 2009 and on October 20, 2010. He assured me that I had nothing to be afraid of in the project since He had given the directives. This is the first leg of my mission. The second leg will come to pass, as the Lord God had foretold. From then on, I started to prepare the materials to write these experiences, and then started writing from December 2010 to December 2011. It was not difficult since I had kept a journal of my spiritual life since 1983, recalling this portion of my life history was easy. It is a good idea to keep a journal of divine and spiritual activities in each person's life. Experienced Church leaders have always advised us to do so.

·◄ CHAPTER 2 ►·

AWESOME GOD

INTRODUCTION

"For the Lord Most high is awesome. He is a great King over all the earth." Psalm 47:2. Now let me share my exciting experiences of the Father with you.

God is spirit. We can only approach Him in the spirit. We can only experience Him in the spirit, but also manifestations occur in the physical body influenced by the spirit. One can experience divine sensations by speaking to the spirit. Suggestions to the heart can be experienced easily. The feeling of a divine 'Presence' can also be sensed in different ways, for example, as a heat, or vibrating or shivering sensation running through one's whole body. One needs to pray immediately covering yourself with the blood of Jesus since I understand that evil spirits also produce a similar sensation in the body.

The sweet smell of flowers around the person, when one cannot visibly see the flowers nearby, indicate a divine presence. Sweet scent of incense also has similar implications when no one around the person is burning incense. Yes, the voice of divine presence speaking loudly or gently in one's ears. Some people are able to see visions, either in parts or in whole, some are able to see future events, either directly or in dreams. A lot of studies have been done about dreams and their meaning. I am convinced that dreams are our portal to the divine and spiritual world if positively channeled. They are also the portal to extra-sensory perception, just as the sensation of 'deja-vu' represents a peep into the future at a time in the past.

I declare here to all that all the Apparitions of the Blessed Mother Mary, which have happened for generations and still do so today, all over the world, are also powerful indications of divine existence, power and authority. Pray through her to God. She's the mother of all.

Furthermore, God speaks to us or touches our needs directly through words spoken to the person directly, or by His Priests/ Pastors, and also from the Holy Bible. Over and over again, the Holy Spirit of God would speak to my heart in response to or about a particular request or clarification I had sought. In the early days of this amazing experience, and to be sure that this was a truly divine experience, I would ask for a specific confirmation, through a specific manner or preaching, a priest's sermon or a preacher on the television. At such periods, the preacher would stop and declare that they were about to digress from the main topic of the day, but nonetheless they would deliver God's message. At other times, they would indicate that although they don't know to whom the specific message was directed, but that God is saying (here they would give my specific feedback) and responding exactly to my issue as I had asked for the confirmation. God encourages us to always test the spirit and be sure to hold onto that which is the spirit of truth. At other times, I would wake up singing a particular song of victory, of thanksgiving, or of adoration. I would sing the complete song as soon as I woke up, but would jot down the song title to enable me to search for the song later. At 5.25a.m on May 11, 2010, I received the song *'Stand Up and Praise the Lord'* by James Montgomery (1824). This was not one of the songs I usually sang or listened to; and at 5.15a.m on Thursday, October 21, 2010, I received another song *'For All the Saints Who from Their Labors Rest'* by William Walsham How (1864). On October 29, 2008, I was woken up and given a whole new song, titled *'Glory to God'*. The four verse song was dictated to me and I wrote the words down. It was a song of divine vindication and favor. I sat speechless but full of joy and gratitude to God. I am still to put these into music, but will do so shortly. These are truly amazing experiences of God in the spirit. I realized through these experiences that God was near, and working in my life, taking me on a journey I didn't fully comprehend, but was totally prepared to follow. At other times, I would pray in my sleep and wake up still praying aloud. From this time on, I became even more devoted and committed to doing His will; no matter what I was facing in the world.

WHAT THE HOLY BIBLE SAYS.

God is eternal, He remains unchanging; the same God yesterday, today and tomorrow. He is "I am that I am," God is the creator of all in heaven, on earth, and the universe. We belong to Him. For man to behave as if we are on our own, or that we are answerable only to ourselves, is shortsighted. His Majesty is explained to us in *1 Chronicle 29:11a&b "Yours O Lord is the greatness, the power and the glory.; the victory and the majesty, for all that is in heaven and on earth is Yours; Yours is the kingdom O Lord, and you are exalted as head over all." The different names of God, some of which are listed here, also tell us who He is. He is Jehovah Jireh, the Lord who provides; Jehovah Rapha the Lord that heals; Jehovah Shammah, the Lord is there; Jehovah Nissi, the Lord my Banner; Jehovah Shalom, the Lord sends peace; Jehovah Raha/Raah, the Lord my shepherd; Jehovah Tsidkenu, the Lord our righteousness; Jehovah El-Shaddai, the Lord who sustains; Jehovah Hullam, the Lord who overcomes. Elsewhere in this book I had also referred to other names by which the Lord God of creation is known by, YHWH or Yaweh, I am; Adonai, Lord/Master; El Elyon, the Most High God; El Elohim, God of Gods/the strong Creator; El Emeth, God of Truth. These listed names here are just but a few of His holy names. Every time we call on His name in all or any form, in holy worship and prayer, He responds to us. Note one thing though, God cannot be mocked or deceived; we must approach Him only with clean hands and pure hearts.*

His works also tell who He is, although these are so many, it is almost futile to list them. In this book, I have however listed what He did for me; His saving grace and power over my life are indeed numerous. *Psalm 40:5 "Many O Lord my God is your wonderful works which you have done . . . ."* One thing I know is that I am one of his wonderful works; a masterpiece of the hand of God, and I know for sure that He has not yet finished with me.

Almighty & Omnipotent God and Father

'I am that I am' was His reply to Moses when Moses wanted to know God's name so He can tell his people when they would question him about who had sent him to free them from bondage. This is said to be a profound, revered name of God among His people, Israel. This and His other names point to the Mighty, all powerful Creator, Unfathomable, Invisible, Loving, Eternal Father, and God. Isaiah 40:1-26 describes in clear details the enormous power of God Almighty, the Holy one, who cannot be likened to anyone known to man.

In the life of turbulence we live, He is our hope and we must totally rest on His powers. *Psalm 71:5 "For you are my hope, O Lord God; You are my trust from my youth." and in* Ephesians 6:10, the Apostle Paul advised us to ". . . be strong in the Lord and in the power of His might."

James 4:7-8 "Therefore submit to God and resist the devil; and he will flee from you. Draw near to God and He will draw near to you . . . ." In these passages, we begin to see the one true way out of demonic afflictions; the sure way to drive Satan, his agents and followers away from us when afflicted; the one way to freedom from bondage.

Divine Power

God's Strength according to Isaiah 41:10, captures one of God's several promises of protection to us. *"Fear not for I am with you. Be not dismayed for I am your God. I will strengthen you, yes I will help you. I will uphold you with my Righteous right hand."* Psalm 18:2 tells us of the saving power of God *"The Lord is my rock and my fortress and my deliverer; My God my strength in whom I will trust; my shield and the horn of my salvation, my strength."* Furthermore, Psalm 27:1a&b tell how God becomes our light when we cannot see clearly. We shall not be afraid because we are resting on God's strength *"The Lord is my light and my salvation; whom shall I fear? The Lord is the strength of my life; of whom shall I be afraid?"*

The Lord's Prayer which we all say often and so very familiarly describes God's Kingdom, Power, and Glory, as well as His many promises of deliverance, salvation, and protection for us. *Matthew 6:13 "And do not lead us into temptation, but deliver us from the evil one. For yours is the Kingdom, and the power, and the glory forever. Amen."*

One of my favorite Bible verses is Psalm 91:1-16. It is the ultimate protection covenant from God for us all, verses 15&16 state *"He shall call upon Me and I will answer him; I will be with him in trouble; I will deliver him and honor him, with long life I will satisfy him; and show him my salvation."* You will recall that God's words are everlasting. Once He had voiced the words, they go out to fulfill His desires, they are sacrosanct.

How He revealed Himself

The unchanging glory of God is eternally displayed all around us. *"The heavens declare the glory of God; and the firmament shows His handiwork." Psalm 19:1*

God is our righteous Champion, quite incomparable to anyone else. He is faithful and loving; shielding us, His own under the shadow of His wings, and caring for us as of new born babies, God delivers us from evil over and over again. He himself is our peace, and so gives and keeps us in perfect peace over and over when our minds are on Him. He showed Himself to us in the covenants He made with us and in the commandments He gave us. He asks that we love Him with all our hearts and remain loyal to Him and walk in His statutes. He showed that He is a jealous God and demands total loyalty, constant attention, and unwavering dedication. His faithfulness is great indeed, and as we all have seen, He remains a forgiving Father. He says that if we walk in the spirit, we will experience Him. This is absolutely so very correct. He asks us to test Him so He can confirm Himself to us. He reveals Himself as a miracle working God over and over again in the lives of men and women. So much so that even some die-hard unbelievers have come to experience Him.

Let me share with you here some of the ways God revealed Himself to me during the period of 'my transition'. Between 2005 and 2012, when recently I had become more aware of His presence and ways, God showed me in different ways what I needed to know. I am now very sure that He was doing this all along, but first my worldliness did not allow me to experience Him, as I needed to. Also, I was so immersed in the crisis of each moment that I didn't really lift my spirit up to experience Him. The situation was destroying me physically, spiritually and mentally. By His loving grace He revealed Himself to me and got through to me. It was an amazing experience. When the holy spirit of God spoke to my heart, just to be sure it was divine voice, I would ask for a specific confirmation, known only to me. He would give the confirmation I asked for. One day in 2010, reviewing my experiences, I was thinking about the real dangers to Priests and Pastors who must face and fight demonic powers regularly for themselves and for their parishioners. Some of these good people are spiritually unprepared for the dangerous work of pastoring, and for the battles they must face. They accept sorcerers, camouflaged witches and wizards into their churches either as itinerant 'worshippers' or as members. These beings often test the Priests, Pastors, and leaders to assess their spiritual powers before they strike. The divine voice said clearly to me *"My people have become servants to witches and wizards, because they do not know and did not ask Me."*

I was stunned! I am sending His message out to all concerned. I know that legislative provisions don't allow churches to discriminate and that churches are considered public places of worship or gatherings, but I also know of some churches where witches would never step into, for fear of exposure. Once exposed, they lose their deadly powers to destroy people, since people would avoid them totally. This is why they operate in total secrecy, cunning and manipulations, pretense, disguise and avoiding the glare of the public. They would destroy anyone if they thought their identities would be discovered. Once they join the churches, they begin to destroy members from within, or recruit new members to their cult. Usually what they cannot control, exploit, or acquire, they destroy often slowly, but sometimes suddenly if it is in their interests to do so. I urge all church leaders to find divine ways to identify, weed out, discourage, and frustrate all evil agents who are currently hiding among the church faithful.

We must remember always that the Almighty God is our 'Shield and Protector' *"For you O God will bless the righteous; with favor you will surround him as with a shield." Psalm 5:12 and in Proverbs 30:5 "Every word of God is pure; He is a shield to those who put their trust in Him."*

FAITHFUL GOD AND FATHER

"There the workers of iniquity have fallen; they have been cast down and are not able to rise." Psalm 36:12. He is constantly protecting us from harm and danger. He defends us against deadly foes. He takes over our battles and fights for us. He is our tower of strength in times of danger, he is our Champion. His right Hand strikes down our enemies forever and they become powerless before our God and Father. *"When my enemies turn back, they shall fall and perish at Your presence." Psalm 9:3.* He is our constant protection. *2 Thessalonians 3:3 "But the Lord is faithful; He will strengthen you and guard you from evil."*

Almighty God teaches us the path we should follow; His path is the path of Righteousness. *"Blessed is the man whom you instruct, O lord. And teach us your law." Psalm 94:12. "Let us hold fast the confession of our hope without wavering; for He who promised is faithful." Hebrews 10:23.* God is our Light. *Psalm 18:28 "For you will light my lamp; The Lord my God will enlighten my darkness."* I understand that evil entities have a way of covering our sight, so that they are not exposed or detected easily. When we can't see, either physically or spiritually, we are incapacitated. The spiritual eyesight sees what others don't see. That one is unable to see what another person sees clearly does not mean that the one is hallucinating. Rather we should be slow to criticize or stereotype, but explore all possible explanations for the unique and insightful vision.

TRUSTING AND WAITING ON GOD.

"Be still and know that I am God; I will be exalted among the nations. I will be exalted in the earth." Psalm 46:10a&b. He is usually exalted from generation to generation and also through His wonderful work and favor to men. Romans 8:31 assures us that God is for us and if so who can be against us. Even if the deadly enemy is very powerful, we should know and trust that the power of God is greater by far. Therefore we should not be distressed when we face the enemy. At the early stages of my battle, I was afraid having seen some examples of the powers of evil.

Then the voice said "Why are you afraid of those who can harm the body but cannot kill the soul?" From then on I became bolder in my God's strength and power. *"The Lord is my portion, says my soul; therefore I hope in Him." Lamentation 3:24.*

As our sanctuary, God promises us safety from harm and danger. The name of the Lord is a strong tower; the righteous run to it and are safe. We are able to experience His safety always when we remain trusting of Him, in whatever circumstance we find ourselves. When the world was falling down all around me, I prayed more, almost fanatically and clung unto Gods feet because my life and sanity depended on Him. My favorite statement always was and is that 'Father I trust you to deliver me from my enemies'. You know what? He did. At one stage, He told me to set my eyes on divine things and goals, and not on earthly things. He said He would strengthen me and uphold me, and He did. When the world called me destructive names, God said those names were not mine; He said I am who He says I am, and He called me biblical names such as Hannah, Victoria, Esther, Sarah, Ruth, Mary, Joy, Favor, Hephzibah a servant, and prophet of God like Melchizedek of old, Blessings, Glory, and Anointed. He said my value is not determined by who people say I am but by what He says I am. *Colossians 3:2 "Set your mind on things from above, not on things on earth." and Psalm 37:4 "Delight yourself also in the Lord and He shall give you the desires of your heart."* 1 Kings 8: 61 also advises us on how to wait on God; *"Let your heart therefore be loyal to the Lord our God, to walk in His statutes, and keep His commandments as at this day."*

⇥ CHAPTER 3 ⇤

SEEKING GOD

INTRODUCTION

I faced prolonged crises of destructive rumors and slander from the early nineteen seventies, while in high school and later in the university, at all the companies where I had worked, and up till the most recent cases reported all over the world. These stories which erupted periodically were strategically timed to humiliate and discredit me in public, to hinder my progress and to destroy my good name and enviable reputation. It took me a while to identify the demonic source of these attacks. Sometime around 1975 and against my advice, Ms. ABCD had abandoned her studies in the third year of a four-year degree course at the university, for reasons best known to her. She then had to live with the consequences of her decision. Apparently she had secretly plotted and executed intensified destructive campaigns of calumny and destruction. When they erupted, I would turn to God in serious prayers, and He would overturn the stories just as He had done in the latest cases and stories which I understand went around the world.

"Draw near to God and He will draw near to you. Cleanse your hands, you sinners; and purify your hearts, you double-minded." James 4:8.

MY STRUGGLES & MORE VICTORIES

In the early days, I didn't have much as I struggled with life and raising my child. So I didn't understand why I was being attacked, slandered, and fought by physical and spiritual forces. The spiritual forces came mostly in the form of dogs, but at other times as lions, tigers, and other wild animals, attacking me or following me or threatening or guarding me, in my dreams over and over again for several years. On one occasion, I dreamt I was held in a caged space in a huge warehouse, as if in prison, and guarded by two dogs. In the dream, I tried to get out but could not. In real life, I was living in an invisible cage, where I could see and speak to others but could never walk into a real life companionship or friendship with males or females, or deep relationships with others around me. As soon as it seemed as if I was forming a relationship with others, the relationship would run into crisis and end. This was one of the ways that witches controlled my life and kept me in bondage. I have had dreams of dogs for as long as I could remember. At first I didn't know who was or were behind these, but eventually in another dream, God showed me who the demonic woman was. First I was afraid, then I went into denial and disbelief, later I spent some years in total shock, because I had opened myself, my family and close contacts to the woman. Once I knew what I was up against, I knew I was in deep trouble; and needed the power of God to become free of bondage. I went to God in prayers, and stepped out of the world. Then God reminded me that he was/ is with me, and I need not fear those who can kill the body but not the soul. *Joshua 1:9 said "Have I not commanded you? Be strong and courageous! Do not tremble or be dismayed, for the Lord your God is with you wherever you go."* You see, truly these words strengthened my faith and all fears disappeared.

Then the Lord God Jehovah rose up in battle like a fierce roaring lion against my enemies. On March 15, 2008, He spoke to me and gave me a covenant of protection when after prayers one day His voice clearly said again: "I am the God of Daniel, the God of Moses and the God of David. I will protect you and defend you from all your enemies." I was so amazed at hearing His voice and so shocked that I couldn't even tell anyone. This was a clear message of war against all my enemies; and I knew they were in for total destruction.

So He fought my battles and destroyed my enemies one by one. Now I understand more. I have also learnt to be still, silent, to measure and time my words, to hold firm to His words in the Holy Bible *"Be still and know that I am God. I will be exalted among the nations. I will be exalted in the earth." Psalm 46:10.* This time the pit which the deadly enemy had dug became her own portion. For anyone out there who is facing similar crises? Pray like a warrior, because God truly lives, the same yesterday, today, and tomorrow.

We cannot see God because He is Spirit. *"God is spirit, and those who worship Him must worship in spirit and in truth." John 4:24.* Unfortunately for people today, "Seeing is believing". I once asked a holy woman how come people today; do not experience God and divine powers as people did in biblical times. She explained that we do not worship God as those people did, without question and in total submission, and concentrating fully, only on God. If we did, she said, we too would experience God as they did. I didn't forget her words. So I tried to do as the Bible tells us, emulating the people in Biblical times. *"When You said 'Seek My face, My heart said to You, 'Your face Lord, I will seek.'" Psalm 27:8.*

The power of God cannot be measured described effectively or comprehended sufficiently. Compared to Him, the enemy is nothing, and can be vanquished just like that. *"And God said to Moses 'I am who I am." Exodus 3:14.*

PRAISE AND WORSHIP

He has commanded us to do several things as His people. One of it is to Praise and Worship Him. Praise Him always for the good He has done for us. *"I will praise You, O Lord, with my whole heart; I will tell of all your marvelous works." Psalm 9:1.* We are to praise Him 24/7, without stopping. *"From the rising of the sun to its going down the Lord's name is to be praised" Psalm 113:3.* *"Come, let us worship and bow down; Let us kneel before the Lord our Maker." Psalm 95:6.* The Holy Bible is full of words of wisdom; one of these is this passage in James 5:13 *"Is any one among you suffering? Let him pray. Is any cheerful? Let him sing praise."*

God Almighty is worthy of our praise since He has drawn us to himself. I love to hear some Christians in Africa call Him 'Daddy'. That name describes closeness to a father; so when we become truly His children, then we have the grace to call Him Daddy. *Psalm 118: 28 tells us "You*

are my God and I will praise you. You are my God and I will exalt you."
Just as we cry and run to our parents, or fathers when in distress, when
the world oppresses us, we have the right to call on Him to fight for us
and give us justice against those who oppress us. He can give justice
more than any other judge. He only holds the power to decide to give
or take vengeance. He sees the innermost workings of man, even where
we could not see, He sees. The secret machinations of man which we do
not know, He knows. *"Rise up, O judge of the earth; Render punishment
to the proud." Psalm 94: 2.* God showed much favor to David partly
because David prayed, worshipped and blessed God, with his entire
soul. *1Chronicles 29:10 "Blessed are You, Lord God of Israel, our Father,
forever and ever".* In the same way, we should openly praise and worship
God without any shame, embarrassment or political correctness. God
is bigger. *"I will sing to the Lord as long as I live; I will sing praise to my
God while I have my being." Psalm 104:33. "Great is the Lord and greatly
to be praised." Psalm 48:1.*

PRAY

"Pray without ceasing." 1 Thessalonica 5:17. Pray without ceasing. It
is such a simple exercise to pray, but somehow it can become a major
challenge for people to get up or kneel down or just to open our mouth
anywhere to pray. I wonder why. Is this lethargy the work of evil forces
working against us and preventing us from accessing God's promises?
Is it just our own carelessness? Are we just being distracted by the world
activities we have to go through every day? I think that if we can see
the evil forces around us, and the damage they do, nothing will hold us
back from praying to God 24/7. God wants us to pray to Him, regularly
and especially in the morning. In *Mark 11:24* He gave His assurances
*"Therefore I say to you ask when you pray, believe that you receive them,
and you will have them."* He particularly appreciates it when we wake
up early to pray to Him, to seek His face, as He promises His special
favor.

*Proverbs 8:34 tells us "Blessed is the man who listens to me, watching daily
at my gates, waiting at the posts of my gates."* This is a beautiful analogy
captured by the **listening, watching, and waiting** on God. Also prayer
needs not have any request. One may just want to stay in the presence

of God in praise, worship, joy, adoration, peace, affection and trusting adulation. That is why we are told that there are different kinds of prayers—Request, Adoration, Supplication, Intercession, Thanksgiving etc. Finally, whatever one's objectives, prayer does work. I have been there.

GIVE THANKS

Over and over again, God instructs us to give thanks. He showed us the value of thanksgiving. He encourages us to do so regularly. In this way He guides us as to how to seek Him. He told us to come before Him with thanksgiving. Many cultures worldwide have institutionalized the practice of 'Thanksgiving' to the Almighty One God. This is one of the great Christian heritage and worthy legacies of the USA. This is a good practice. *"Let us come before His presence with thanksgiving; Let us shout joyfully to Him with psalms." Psalm 95:2. "To the end that my glory may sing praise to You and not be silent, O lord my God, I will give thanks to you forever." Psalm 30:12.* I was amazed when sometime in 2011; I was planning an annual thanksgiving in a certain manner, when I was gently advised to take the thanksgiving in a slightly different form. It was such a clear instruction that I was not in doubt the Lord God Jehovah wished it that way. This is not unusual you know, He speaks to us from time to time; but the world's bustling distractions continue to hinder us from hearing or sensing His presence or knowing He is there with us always. That is why I will say as in *Psalm 89:1 "I will sing of the mercies of the Lord forever; with my mouth will I make known your faithfulness to all generations."* Do you know that the more you give Him thanks, the more He gives you reasons to thank Him? It's an amazing phenomenon, you should try it.

IN HIS HOLY PRESENCE

When we are before Him, even though we cannot see Him, He is present. He has ways of showing us His presence. It could be a sensation of cold, a sensation of heat, quietness all around, a peaceful presence around us. A sense one is not alone. He tells us how to comport ourselves in His presence. *"Oh come let us worship and bow down; Let us kneel before the Lord our Maker." Psalm 95:6.*

In His presence we should show all manner of respect, an acknowledgement of His Holiness and to honor Him. When I relocated to the US, I attended a church where women did not cover their heads in church, a general cultural practice. This is different from my experiences and the practices in the UK and in Africa where it was culturally expected to cover the head in church with a Sunday hat or head-tie. So I wanted to blend in, do as they do in Rome, so to speak, and not draw any attention to myself by a head scarf. Ironically, the fact that I displayed my hair/ head somehow became one of the reasons stories began to circulate among some female congregation members. So I didn't blend in; I thought it was due to a combination of factors, my height and full head of hair, or other reasons? I didn't know. I actually sought divine guidance in prayer and one day I opened my bible to *1 Corinthians 11:1-34*, where I understood that a covered head is a sign of respect for God; it is not just mere convenient fashion. I was further convinced that God was talking to me, answering my specific questions and resolving my dilemma. Thereafter I continued to cover my head in His presence wherever I went to church, never mind what the Romans do in Rome. When you are in His presence, there is a calm aura, a bodily physical sensation through one's body; there is joy and fullness of life. One comes alive with every fiber of the body rising to honor Him. At that time, when you listen hard enough, closing yourself to external noises and fully concentrating on God, you will hear Him speak to your inner person; a suggestion is placed in your heart; there is contentment in your soul, and your spirit is satisfied.

LOVE GOD

"I will love you O Lord my strength." Psalm 18:1. This is a declaration of unquestioned love, total affection and loyalty, above whatever business we are involved in, above whomsoever we are involved with. This is total love for the one who upholds us; the one who sustains us; the one who gave us life. *Proverbs 8:13 "To love God is to hate evil . . . ."* in this famous passage, there are no grey areas. As the love for God takes over one's life, the Holy Spirit instructs the person to avoid all that is ungodly, all that is evil and against the holiness of God. This transformation will affect all areas of life, so much so that one can no longer live the former lifestyle. Do you know that the Bible anticipated this situation and instructs that we choose God against all others? There is really no other choice.

In some of their sermons, Christian Preachers have described these experiences as going into another level of destiny. The friends, family members and contacts that one leaves behind are not necessarily bad people; they are not destined to be with that person in the new journey, as the person walks towards his life's destiny. Our Father made us a promise in *Proverbs 8:17* "*I love those who love me; those who seek me early morning will find me.*" The crises I faced forced me to seek Him and to hold on to Him since there was no one around who even knew, understood or believed the attacks of sorcery I was going through; and as He revealed Himself to me I have come to love Him even more dearly than ever before. These men of God also confirmed and I discovered that no matter how strong the enemies are, no matter how bad the situation is, no matter how high the mountains are God is stronger, greater, and bigger. He spoke in a quiet voice saying "*I am with you. Do not fear those who can kill the flesh but cannot kill the soul.*" If anyone ever doubted God exist, don't doubt any longer. He truly lives. He is God yesterday, today and tomorrow.

KEEPING HIS COMMANDMENTS

Over and over again God tells us to keep His commandments. His Commandments are many, but mostly these ten are well recognized, recommended from the time of Moses and widely used by all humanity. *Deuteronomy 5:6-21.* As a reminder, I am listing the commandments here again, but in summary form.

1. I am the Lord your God, you shall have no other gods before me.
2. Thou shall not make for yourself, graven images or worship idols. I am a jealous God.
3. You shall not take the name of the Lord your God in vain
4. Observe the Sabbath day and keep it holy.
5. Honor your Father and Mother.
6. Thou shall not kill
7. Thou shall not commit adultery
8. Thou shall not steal
9. Thou shall not bear false witness against your neighbor
10. Thou shall not covert your neighbor's wife or his property.

It is in doing this that one knows that one loves God, that one learns to live in His holy presence, with thanksgiving in your heart for His unending love and care. In doing this, praying to God becomes an enjoyable life experience which one seeks over and over again, welcoming every opportunity to approach Him in prayerful communication. Praise and worship come easily, all day, everywhere, even in sleep, to the person, as your conscious and subconscious mind reflect continually over His majesty, affection, care, and continued presence in your life. When God is with you, the person is truly favored; you become the apple of His eyes. It is an experience for which my words are inadequate to describe effectively. It is an experience which must be lived. He guides one every step of one's life, His arms are around the person; He tends one so closely as if the person is the only person on earth. He forgives our sins and encourages us into righteous conduct. Awesome God! Give us your grace to keep your laws throughout our lives.

TRUST GOD

Truly there are times when He will virtually command a person to come to Him over the waters. One must trust Him and His powers to save; abandon all safety nets and walk to Him. Even when He has not shown one any obvious signs of His presence, one knows He is there. When He says something, trust He will do it, so much so that when one lives in His presence, one stops asking for things. He then begins to invite the person to enjoy His fullness. *"The earth is the Lord's and its fullness thereof and all that dwell therein." Psalm 24:1.* In this His assurance, our interest in mundane pleasures of the world wane. This is what the bible was saying by storing heavenly riches. When there are delays or if the request is not answered, my priests have said it is possible that what one asked for was not in one's interest, or maybe God is planning a better deal for the person. I have found both to be true. We must trust God absolutely. In times of danger, we must remember His all-powerful presence and release all battles, wars, temptations, fears, and aspirations totally to him. By the time we have come this far with God, we are truly dwelling in the secret place of the Most High God—His heart. Nothing evil can touch us at this time. We are surrounded by His presence, His power, His love, His protection, His eyes, His Spirit. Remember I am sharing experiences, not preaching. I am unqualified and untrained to preach; but have His mandate to tell the world what He has done. *"Blessed is the man who trusts in the Lord, and whose hope is in the Lord."* *Jeremiah 17:7,* such a person lives in perpetual peace. *"You will keep him in perfect peace, whose mind is stayed on You, because he trusts in You. Trust in the Lord forever; For in Yah, the Lord is everlasting strength."* *Isaiah 26:3&4.*

". . . He is our peace, who has made us both one, and has broken down the dividing wall of hostility." Ephesians 2:14. Over the years and as I stand up to overcome life's challenges, I call on the Lord to come down and uphold me. Remember He is a God of justice, He upholds the weak so that the weak can say I am strong. Against the formidable power of God, sorcerers who are agents of Satan in all their activities, become confused and totally incapacitated. When we wrestle with principalities and wicked peoples in high and low places, our mere flesh is insufficient to combat the enemy. But call on God, Father, Son, and Holy Spirit, and see the enemies scatter in defeat and confusion. *"The Lord is my rock and my fortress and my deliverer; My God my strength, in whom I will trust; My shield and the horn of my salvation, my stronghold." Psalm 18:2.* When we are tempted or in danger dear Lord, I pray that You keep us trusting You. Amen.

SERVE GOD

A respected Christian Preacher once explained that when God invites you into His special favor in the ways described above, He has a special purpose for one and for that relationship, and it is that special divine mark. In most cases, there is a divine mission involved. So the Holy Spirit begins to guide and prepare the person for that mission. We also know that whatever assignment that God gives to man, He stays with the person to fulfill it. It is true He seeks out arms and legs to carry out His ground work. To be chosen to serve the Father is the highest honor any human can aspire to; experienced preachers have explained though, that God picks and choses whosoever He wishes to do His holy will on earth. Other Preachers also warned that demonic agents will attack such a person fiercely, but no matter their antics, God will prevail. As one seeks God's will first in life, He then shows us more favor than one can imagine. I am still counting all the goodness of God to me, if I have a million fingers they are not enough to list them all. If I start talking about them, I will talk for the rest of my life about God and His mercies. *"Delight yourself also in the Lord, and He shall give you the desires of your heart." Psalm 37:4.* We all know the traditional ways in which people serve God—usually in the Priestly calling, the Religious life, or in humanitarian activities. In 1978, I worked with a truly Christian professional leader and boss who introduced me to the Opus Dei society and their wonderful doctrine—simply serving God where one is, in the daily work or employment where one is, and by working to one's best, as well as offering this service to God; this enables one to so honor God in that daily work. This became a profound motto which had guided me throughout my professional carrier and into my private life. That boss took on the role of a spiritual father for me ever since. Although I have lost touch with him since his retirement, I have continued to keep him in the highest regard. I'm passing this on to others as well. Serve and honor God in our simple daily life and activities. Such higher ideals are truly satisfying to the body and soul. In recent times, Management theories have also come round to the knowledge that human motivation is mostly inner directed, that inner direction is from the person's spirit. The organization may give a conducive environment or maybe not, but the main ingredient for motivation and excellence is internally derived. Also those of us, who are parents, were entrusted with raising another human being positively. As my daughter has often said, there are no manuals, so to speak, for doing this successfully; however, raising our children is an important way in which we serve God. My Priests have often taught that apart from the Religious Calling, raising children in the love of God, in the will of God, is another major way to serve God. I have operated with a belief that each person on earth, has been put here to touch the lives of others with whom we interact at various stages of our earthly journey, in a positive manner. In fact, I go as far as saying that the individual gifts God gave us were given, so as to use them positively to touch others. Every day, I ask Him to help me to do this successfully.

--- ⊰ CHAPTER 4 ⊱ ---

JESUS CHRIST, DIVINE SON

INTRODUCTION

Christ truly died for us in all ramifications, in all spheres of existence. In that death He overcame sin, the devil, demons, witches, wizards, and satanic powers. He is the name above all names, the overcomer of all antagonists, the conqueror of all evil forces, and the champion of Christians. Let me correct that; the champions of true Christians. There are many entities who attend different churches as members, who donate generously to charities, who are in all the church societies, guilds, ministries, and committees, who attend church services daily and every Sunday and yet leave the services to go in the way of their demons. If this piece reads like or sounds like I am preaching, that is not my mission. My mission is to declare here that God the Father, Son and Holy Spirit cannot be mocked. I realize that these elements really don't know or believe in God or in His commandments or in His immense powers. They rather believe in the power of Pharaoh and the chariots of Pharaoh. Their experiences with me had baffled them because they look for the source of my strength, and although I had declared loudly to those near to me over the years, that God is my strength, they didn't still believe, they kept on testing God's power, thinking they were testing me. God once said to me, *"I am with you."* This is a statement God frequently used in the bible, about three hundred and sixty five times in all. He does so whenever His own anointed people are in any danger, or are afraid because of the enemy. Therefore if God be with us, who can be against us? *Deuteronomy 31:6* says *"Be strong and of good courage, do not fear or be in dread of them: for it is the Lord your God who goes with you; He will be with you, He will not fail you or forsake you; do not fear or be dismayed."* To all who are reading this, the promise of God remains constant and valid, when we face trials and tribulations instigated by the world. *"Fear not, for I am with you, be not dismayed for I am your God; I will strengthen you, I will help you, I will uphold you with my victorious right hand." Isaiah 41:10.* The right hand of God is universally acclaimed as the hand of Justice for the oppressed, and feared by all enemies of God.

What the Holy Bible says

"Jesus is the way, the truth and the light. He is the Word of God, who was before all time began. He is the Prince of peace, the King of Kings, the Savior of the world." Psalm 34:8 & Psalm 107:29. Just as He calmed the sea in those years, He still calms the stormy seas of our lives. He came to free us from evil, from ourselves and from sin; He fought and overcame Satan for us, and earned us the right to be called the children of God. He was the Teacher, Messiah; He who rewards all good deeds.

Therefore let us all *". . . give thanks to God who gives us the victory through our Lord Jesus Christ." 1 Corinthians 15: 57. Hebrews 10:23* assures us *"Let us hold fast the confession of our hope without wavering, for He who promised is faithful."* I tell you during these trying times, I was tested but the grace of God remained my strength; and when Jesus Christ took over the battle, I was totally relieved. *Matthew 16:27; "For the Son of man is to come with His angels in the glory of His Father, and then he will repay every man for what he has done." "Behold He is coming with the clouds, and every eye will see him, everyone who pierced him; and all tribes of the earth will wail on account of him; Even so. Amen." Revelation 1:7.* I assure you all that every word of the Holy Bible is true. Every promise of God is sacrosanct. It is the "Word" of God, in both the spiritual form and the physical form, which has remained our shield against demonic attacks. You see, God warned that we in our physical state are no match for demonic forces. When we hand over the battle to Jesus, we easily overcome. Do the same in your own life.

JESUS CHRIST THE WAY

It is for these reasons that we need Jesus in all areas of life. When I recall my years of innocence, of blindly trusting, the years of naivety, stumbling from crisis to crises, and talking to those who caused the crises never realizing whom I was talking to; if not for the grace of God that led me to Jesus Christ the Way, I was amazed that I have survived and lived. For several years, I was walking in total disorientation. I know now that the Lord had a purpose for my life. I will fulfill that purpose by His grace. In John 14:16, Jesus said to Thomas the Apostle, *"I am the way, the truth and the life; no one comes to the Father, but by me . . . ."* I had recounted elsewhere in this book how Our Mother, the Blessed Virgin Mary, had guided me to go to Jesus Christ "The Way" towards resolving the destructive demonic attacks I had faced. The minute I handed over my problems to God, I became free of tension, of anxiety, of pain, of persecution, of humiliation, of the war of tongues and disorientation. I had something to hold onto, it was the Son of God, Jesus Christ. It was that focus that sustained me. I tell you there is a lot going on in the spiritual world, unseen and unknown by us. We see the effect on our physical state of being, but can't understand the processes which had occurred in that spiritual sphere giving us the result in our world. It is this missing link that people in today's world refer to as divine intervention. Conversely, in other situations the spiritual attack appears as abnormal behavior in the physical world which leads to the labeling of the person, though wrongly. I became a new creation in Christ, once I found the way through the grace of God.

2 Corinthians 5:17 says, "Therefore if anyone is in Christ, he is a new creation; the old has passed away, behold the new has come." I like the new by far. Everyone who seeks Christ seeks the light and the way.

THE DIVINE HEALER

The healing miracles of Jesus confirmed His divinity without doubt. The Holy Bible is filled with his miracles from the feeding; the marriage miracles of turning water into wine, to the healing of the sick, to the victories over demonic entities, curing the lame, the sick, the lepers, to his bringing the dead to life, His own resurrection from death to life. After

His Ascension into heaven, his disciples continued to perform miracles in His name. Today the Churches are filled with divine miracles of Mary His mother, who had since become the divine Messenger following the descent of the Holy Spirit on Pentecost. Jesus healed in the body, the spirit and the soul. In my own case He also healed me totally. When the enemies attacked my eyes I felt it by sensations of sharp pin pricks several times. I considered these sensations unusual at the time and because the Holy Spirit was with me, He called my attention to the events being demonic attacks. So I called onto the blood of Jesus and His name and He healed me so much so that I now have a nearly 20/20 vision as confirmed by my Optometrist in October 2011; whereas I used to wear heavy prescription glasses and contact lenses. Recently I was able to thread the needle to do some sewing quite easily, whereas I used to ask younger persons to do that for me. He had healed me also of demonic fear, anxiety, tension, headaches, poisoning, and all manner of health afflictions. Just as all physical illnesses are not necessarily demonic in nature, so also are they not all physical in nature. It is wise to treat these health problems from both the physical and spiritual dimensions. I have watched amazing recounts of divine healing on the television stations. The most beautiful aspect of healing is that in Luke 11:9-10, Jesus tells us just what we simply need to do. *"And I tell you, ask and it will be given you; seek, and you will find; knock and it will be opened to you. For everyone who asks receives, and he who seeks, finds and to him who knocks, it will be opened."*

THE REDEEMING LAMB

When one prays, call on the ***Blood of Jesus*** shed on the cross to redeem us from Satan's powers. That blood still has powers, even till today. We actually recall the Passion of Christ, where His blood was shed for our redemption. That redemption was and is total. Once recalled, the blood rises up again and again to destroy the enemy. Do not go out without the precious Blood of Jesus Christ, the redeeming Lamb of God. In prayer warfare, when one calls on the Blood to come forth on your behalf, He responds.

Recall also that when the soldiers pierced the side of Jesus, His precious bodily Water was spilled. ***The Water of Jesus*** was shed to wash us clean (of demonic mud, dirt, stains, sins, tension, pain, afflictions, etc.). This Water of Jesus is a cleanser for our spirit and soul. In 2009 soon after I relocated to the United States, I had a dream in which I saw Ms. ABCD who was also visiting the country, standing next to me in that dream; and suddenly she pushed me into a river of mud, thick brown mud, I couldn't get any foothold in the slippery mud, and as I began to sink, I called on the name of Jesus to save me. Immediately I started to emerge from the mud and walked out covered in mud. I woke up and understood clearly the muddy attack. So I asked Jesus to wash me with the waters flowing from His side and to make me clean. He did. Every story of the War of tongues which was meant to smear me and to destroy my name was represented by the muddy encounter. By the Water of Jesus, I was washed clean and vindicated over and over again, much to the shame of my enemies and detractors. Oh! Thank God for the cleansing Water from the side of Jesus. Furthermore, the mud prepared by the demonic agents became their portion. How the Lord did it is a spiritual miracle. Mine is to thank Him. Yours is to pray always using the Blood and Water of Jesus.

The Spirit of Jesus Christ lives on in all true Christians, making the demonic agents around cringe at His name and spirit in us, His followers. That Spirit is still alive and working on earth. You see the third element which was shed on Calvary for us by Jesus, was His Spirit. In fact, it was the concluding item of His Passion, when He released His Spirit to His Father. As the spirit returned to God, it shook the earth causing earthquake, it tore the buildings, the temple was shaken, the tornado was fierce. All these were consequences of the divine energy released at that point in the death of Jesus Christ at 3p.m. on that Holy Friday. It is that power which we call upon to our aid in battle. It is for this reason that 3p.m. prayers are very powerful. This period is also known as the period of great divine Mercy. So pray especially at this time and call on the spirit of Christ to rise up again and fight for you. I do not claim to have explanations as to '*how*', but just my testimony that it works and had done so in my case. Upon my relocation to the US, one of the Prayer groups I sought out and joined was the group which prays at 3p.m. regularly both in homes and in the church. This is the hour during which the Catholic Church prays **the Chaplet of the Divine Mercy,** whomsoever you are and wherever you are find the prayer session and join in this, or other similar prayers at 3p.m. daily. At the end, make your request to God.

The Sacred Heart of Jesus

The preceding write up leads me to the Sacred Heart of Jesus. You will recall that I went to the Shrine of the Sacred Heart Catholic Cathedral, on Sacred Heart Street, off 16th Street N.W. Washington D.C. At the church and in the presence of God, I had asked for His Divine intervention and the help of the Blessed Virgin Mother Mary. Truly Jesus Christ is the friend of man. He died to save us because He loved us so much that everywhere He saw human misery, His first response is to relieve it. The heart of Jesus is the sure sanctuary for us to run to in danger. In all my writing, I give others the guide to find succor and relief in the same way as I did. Cling to the heart of Jesus in prayers, in songs, in thoughts and in your deeds and you will be victorious.

Jesus Christ is the divine Teacher, teaching us from the time He was 12 years old, some say even earlier, till the end of His first earthly dwelling. He taught in the morning, afternoon, evening, night time, all the time; and everywhere He went. Jesus taught the Rabbi, Pharisees, the Apostles, His disciples, the multitudes which followed Him and even His enemies. Today the writings of His Apostles continue to teach, guide, and heal us. The Holy Bible is a living document, do not read it as a historical account, but read it, use it, invoke God's powers hidden in it even when we don't know how that is, but in total trust and faith, we use the Holy Bible and ask Jesus to teach us what specific things we need to know in our specific case. What specific steps we need to take or follow in our specific challenge. At other times, we should remind Him of His teachings and the promises in those teachings to solve our particular case. Knowing what is in the heart of the person afflicted, when we go to God in faith and in total surrender, and as we open our Holy Bible, God the Father, Son, and Holy Spirit tells us what we need to know with full understanding of the teachings in the Bible. Going further, Priests, Pastors, and true Messengers of Christ still speak and teach us His messages and lessons even today. Listen attentively to what they are saying and learn from them.

Jesus Christ is the true Shepherd. *John 10:11 "I am the good Shepherd. The Good shepherd lays down his life for the sheep."* He will always keep the ninety-nine safe and then go after the one missing or lost one so as to bring it to safety. Many people have been misled into thinking that the powers which the satanic agents offer is what one needs to live successfully. They won't tell you the dastardly consequences of such a venture, both on earth and at the end of life. Sometimes, earthly problems are caused by satanic agents just so as to frustrate the child of God and to push him or her into the cult of Satan. Remember, just as we are awaiting the return of Christ, so also are these deadly agents campaigning to increase their numbers, and the number of souls to destroy prior to that second coming. The only problem is that they would deceive, lie, and use cunning, subterfuge, and misrepresentations to attract victims. In the present culture of silence about demonic forces at work in the world, many innocents have come to be enticed into evil cults without realizing what they were in to. Follow Jesus, the true shepherd, no one else. Unfortunately, modern media culture has openly glamourized the satanic, demonic, and evil forces showing up with much dollar success on our screens, fame, and glitter; thus creating the deliberate dangerous attraction to both young and old. When we then combine the power of advertisement with the unexplainable silence of the people of God about the dangers posed by satanic attraction, it is no wonder that innocent people are easily attracted into demonic cults.

These evils they portray on the television are very similar to the destruction they inflict on the lives of ordinary persons without divine spiritual support. Believe me the same evils perpetrated by these beings on the ground are as deadly. Our only lasting hope is Jesus Christ the Shepherd.

FOLLOWING JESUS CHRIST

In the world of total darkness in which we live, it is only by the light of Christ that we are able to see our way, and navigate our life's journeys. *John 8:12, "Then Jesus spoke to them again saying I am the light of the world. He who follows me shall not walk in darkness, but have the light of life."*

The holy Bible tells us that Jesus Christ the Light will return, and all of us Christians are preparing for that return. Between now and then, Christians try to live Christ-like lives. Being a Christian is very difficult indeed. We will have to choose between the world habits and the divine. One may lose friends, family and possibly increase foes. Every trial of Christ, you too will experience though in a minute manner, although that minuteness would appear huge to us. Preachers have taught us to expect persecution of all types, to expect slander, antagonism, mud slings, etc. When this happens, offer these sufferings to the Lord and rest assured that we are on the right path. Let us remember that our path to our respective destiny is totally separate from the path of others. Furthermore, only we must follow our path, each person must follow their own paths to their destinies. In the recent experience I had, I was very concerned at a stage that I was losing all the friends I had acquired over the years. One by one, friends started to abandon me, some openly fought with me, and others fought me covertly and abandoned me. Then I heard a southern charismatic Preacher explain that these are common developments as we each journey to our respective destinations and destinies. Most friendships are merely for a while, when people's paths cross and separate. It doesn't mean that they are evil or that you are evil, it is just time to go separate ways, sometimes in peace, and sometimes in discord. Furthermore, all those departures were never meant to be part of the future of the new person. So we need to expect and even welcome departures from time to time, but wish all kindness in their future, but thank God for the learning and growth that inevitably happen to the person, in the individual's life's journey. Everywhere Christ went, He touched others positively, going good.

For several years in my adult life, I had held on to the philosophy that each of us was put on this earth to touch the lives of others positively. I must have received this by God's grace and inspiration by the Holy Spirit. Touching others positively became the driving ethos in my life. You will recall that I was going through major challenges and experiencing difficulties. I would then tell God that if I touched others in positive ways, He must surely touch mine also positively. The more I suffered in the hands of my oppressors, the harder I looked for opportunities to reach out and touched others. Along the way, I discovered that there is intrinsic joy in the act of supporting others when we see them emerge a better, prosperous, successful, progressive, happier, more peaceful person. It gave me great joy to reach out and touch others. So the act became itself a motivation to do more and more. I thank God for the opportunities He gave me to do the things I did. I found out that it also took my focus off my problems as I concentrated on the needs of others. I suppose this therapy was also good for me. Perhaps one may wish to do like Christ, do as much good as one can, all the time. We are building our spiritual bank account in heaven. Our Father sees all, and will repay all our good deeds.

---⊰ CHAPTER 5 ⊱---

THE HOLY SPIRIT

INTRODUCTION

"The Spirit of God has made me. And the breath of the Almighty gives me life." Job 33:4. We operate in a multi-dimensional world. Our five or even six senses are inadequate to understand, to process, to manage and to respond adequately to our environment, and all the stimuli. Consider the simple concept of Perception, even with the ordinary senses, what we each perceive, and how we process that perception is as diverse as the human race. This diversity has led to diverse interpretations and subsequent actions, responses and behaviors. Now compound that with the extra sensory perception and divine perception. Somehow, I was able to see a lot more than meets the eye, than others around me from the time the Lord began to show me what I needed to see around me, when I started to know things revealed only by the Holy Spirit. Different people around me became different entities, and for the first time I saw them as they really are. I really didn't see or know these individuals before my eyes became opened. I also saw situations in whole, not in parts, and the whole that I saw was certainly more than the sum of the parts. The Spirit of God is really an amazing experience. I now know that all mankind, without the grace to see beyond the five senses are definitely at a disadvantage, working blindly and therefore responding inadequately. I can fully appreciate the situation of the blessed Apostle Paul when God opened his eyes and he saw differently. When this happened, he became a different person, much to the shock of others around him. I was truly blind but now see. My eyes were opened by the grace of God.

From *my experiences*, I confirm that the Holy Spirit wakes me up in the mornings at the time am expected to meet the Father in prayers even if I don't use my alarm clock. He prompts me about life, dangers, and victories. He uses songs to guide me. I may just burst into a particular song subconsciously and He tells me to listen to the song the hymn, when I do, He has a message for me. In my dreams I can now tell when danger is near and what danger is lurking. When I do something wrong He tells me I was wrong. When I feel down and somewhat frustrated, He lifts me up either with word from the Holy bible, from Preachers around me, or by speaking to my ears uplifting words of encouragement. On the occasions I ask God for answers, the Spirit responds to me. When I was about to make an unwise social investment, He warned me in a dream, the day before. Unfortunately I didn't see the connection at the time, so I ignored that dream only to see it a few days after. I learnt my lessons and now understand and ask Him first.

WHAT THE HOLY BIBLE SAYS

Once one has tested and confirmed the presence of the Holy Spirit in one's life, one begins to experience a companionship which is indescribable. The experience is amazing and out of this world, because one no longer walks blind, rather one walks with confidence and assurance, that one walks with God and walk aright. *"For the kingdom of God is not eating and drinking, but righteousness and peace and joy in the Holy Spirit." Romans 14:17.* Most of us have been at crossroads in our lives. Others have also been through trials, tribulations and major challenges of life. It is at such times that we turn to God because there is just no one else we can trust. Friends disappear, families disown, neighbors shut their doors/windows quickly, but the Holy Spirit of God remains with you. Anyone who seeks the Lord God Father, Son, and Holy Spirit truthfully will find Him. *"And you will seek Me and find Me, when you search for Me with all your heart." Jeremiah 29:13.* A useful bible passage, calling on the Holy Spirit to guide one's path, one's ways and one's life daily. Frankly, there is no other way. *Psalm 143:8 "Cause me to hear Your loving kindness in the morning. For in You do I trust; Cause me to know the way in which I should walk; For I lift up my soul to You." Colossians 3:2. "Set your sight on things above, not on things on the earth."* The Holy Spirit was so alive in the life of St. Paul; he transformed the church of

Christ on earth. The apostolic work he did with the Holy Spirit as guide, carried the gospel message to the ends of the world, and still lives on today. In most of his messages, he often referred to the inspiration he received from the Holy Spirit. At other times he spoke of the work of the Holy Spirit in the church; and he often counseled his congregation to seek the guidance of the Holy Spirit in all their endeavors. St. Peter and the other Apostles became greatly transformed beings on account of the Holy Spirit. Pray therefore for the Holy Spirit in our lives so that we too might become truly transformed. Please do not seek demonic spirit, for although these have some elements of power, their power is self-destructive in the long run. It is not constructive but evil and ungodly; also they cannot save. So that when they are confronted by the Holy Spirit they disintegrate into nothingness. Like *Job 33:4, I also say that "the Spirit of God made me, and the breath of the Almighty gives me life."* Rather than destroy my spirit or my life the enemies have failed woefully because I have the grace of God. *"You have granted me life and favor; And your care has preserved my spirit." Job 10:12.*

Manifestations of the Spirit

We know the Holy Spirit through the fruits it yields. *"But we know the fruit of the Spirit is love, joy, peace, longsuffering, kindness, goodness, faithfulness, gentleness, self-control. Against such there is no law."* Galatians 5: 22-23. The Holy Bible also said at the same time that to be in the spirit, one needs to overcome the desires of the flesh, the passions of the world, in short moderation and self-denial in all our conduct. *"And those who are in Christ have crucified the flesh with its passions and desires. If we live in the spirit, let us also walk in the spirit." Galatians 5:24-2.5*

St. Paul's letter in Ephesians 5:8-13 speaks clearly about the effect of the Holy Spirit of God, the spirit of darkness, our conduct and sacred duties in these relationships. He condemns these nefarious activities openly and advised all true Christians to follow the light of Christ. *"For you were once darkness, but now you are light in the Lord. Walk as children of light, (for the fruit of the Spirit is in all goodness, righteousness and truth), finding out what is acceptable to the Lord. And have no fellowship with the unfruitful works of darkness, but rather* **expose them***; for it is shameful* *even to speak of those things which are done by them in secret. But all things that are exposed are made manifest by the light, for whatever makes manifest is light."* One cannot really be a true child of the Light, a child of Christ and have or share any relationship whatsoever with demonic or satanic beings. Light will always cover darkness and show what is hidden in darkness. Unfortunately many people still pretend to be Christians; they put up shows of pseudo-Christian conduct but really belong to satanic darkness. To complete their charade, they seek the company and cloak of piety and good conduct only to turn round at night and fly like the demonic birds that they are, destroying unsuspecting lives, deceiving their innocent victims, stealing goodness from people, spreading destruction, and pain in the world. *Ephesians 6:10-12* tells us further what to do in order to overcome the world of evil around us, *"Finally my brethren, be strong in the Lord and in the power of His might. Put on the whole armor of God that you may be able to stand against the wiles of the devil; for we do not wrestle against flesh and blood, but against principalities, against powers, against the rulers of the darkness of this age, against spiritual host of wickedness in the heavenly places. Therefore put on the armor of God . . . ."* Dear readers, these evil beings are everywhere around us, in homes, in schools, in churches, in eating places, in dance halls, in work places, in buses, in trains, in the neighborhood, at social gatherings, and the list goes on. They mix with normal people and pretend to be saintly; they are quiet and try to be unobtrusive as they wreak havoc on innocent lives. God help us.

ROLES OF THE HOLY SPIRIT

Wisdom—In Daniel 2:20 *"Daniel said, Blessed be the name of God for ever and ever, to whom belong wisdom and might."* We cannot see many things going on around us, in our lives, to others near us, and we are literally blind to demonic activities and influences in our lives until the Holy Spirit gives us the gifts of Wisdom, Knowledge, and Understanding. The world takes on a different perspective. Once we have the spirit to see, know, and discern the spiritual world around our physical world, we become a different person. That is why the concept of Perception as reality is so very true. We react and respond to what we see, what we know. If you don't know, your response will be either lethargic, none or misdirected. In this situation, those who have spiritual or the negative demonic powers have a field day. The evil ones rope and bound the innocent completely while they smile to the person, while they destroy the person at the same time as they ask you for help, favors and support in one way or another. They know you are ignorant and so do maximum damage at your expense. Pray therefore like Solomon for the power of Wisdom. Proverbs also guide us excellently in the path of wisdom. Read both books, pray for wisdom, and become wiser.

Knowledge—The knowledge given us by the spirit enables us to prepare ourselves better for battle, to direct our prayers and energy appropriately. Divine knowledge comes to us from the spirit. You get to know things as they are deposited in your heart. Test them out as the Holy Bible advises us to and you will find shocking revelations, hitherto unknown to one. At a meeting where I was present, two people who had been fiddling with the organizational funds were exposed by the Holy Spirit. The company Accountant had just completed presenting the Accounts and Reports to the meeting and had successfully answered all questions. Knowing that few members paid detailed attention to the specifics of the presentations, and since the Auditor would have gone over the books of accounts and attested to the fact of its accuracy; no one paid much detailed attention to the figures. At a specific point in time and just as two key members of a fraud group exchanged very brief knowing glances, the Holy Spirit took my attention to them; and I knew the glances were significant and eventually found that they were fiddling with funds and cooking the books, banking on the trust of the entire membership. This exposure and subsequent re-audits showed up unprecedented fraud in both local and foreign currency transactions of the small firm. Truly, the Holy Spirit gives knowledge, especially the ability to know secret things, secret plans, and secret steps of others who may wish to harm you. Knowledge also comes in dreams. Never dismiss your dreams as useless. Explore their messages, seek divine clarifications if need be, but don't rest easy until you have knowledge.

Understanding—This came for me when I was able to put all the pieces together through the power of the Holy Spirit; I saw the whole picture and understood my situation better. We see individual scenes and pieces of the puzzle, sometimes never able to understand the full extent and ramifications. Also, the Holy Spirit has taught me to ask why? Every human action has a reason; every human reaction has a goal and a purpose. Most times we may make assumptions about others' actions and comments, but as we learnt to listen more and ask the question why both of the opponent and of oneself, then the answers begin to come out. Also an adult can often tell when the other party is lying, or hiding something, or giving half-truths. Polite culture may prevent one from declaring such lies openly; but one knows. Follow your instincts, beware, and be on guard. Be careful at taking face-value answers as deep truths. Test every important statement. Most often the world around us distracts us from looking, thinking or examining issues deeply by asking the question, why? *"For the kingdom of God is not food and drink but righteousness and peace and joy in the Holy Spirit." Romans 14:17.*

Bearing divine messages—The Holy Spirit has continued to carry divine messages from God to the world, to people and to countries, appearing in forms of people, angels, even the divine dove. We are lucky to have this connection promised and released to the world as Jesus was to return to the Father. The world has literally been taken over by demonic and satanic forces; so much so that the woman sleeping next to an innocent husband may be a witch and he would never know unless and until the Holy Spirit tells him. The neighbor living next door and their daughter or son who plays with yours and attend school with your children could be senior witches and wizards. I have seen and heard on televised 'Deliverance' services where young children would come out to renounce the devil and in that process confess their past deadly activities as satanic agents. The sweet single attractive girl who a man picks up in a bar or at a party could be a witch, who would cause much pain and destruction in the man's home, marriage, and life. The most frightening thing is that the poor man at this time is under the total control and demonic influence of the woman who dictates and directs his entire life, although he and others around would never suspect who was really the person in charge. The Holy Spirit reveals hidden secrets and carries information and messages to the person whom God wants to favor. His message could come as a human voice; it could come as a specific reply to one's specific prayer request; it could come as a dream, it could come as a physical sensation to the body. One thing I know is that messages from the Holy Spirit come clear, loud, directly and are unmistakable. The ultimate goal is to make the life of the person better, fuller, safer, healthier and more peaceful.

CONNECTING TO THE HOLY SPIRIT

One of my real life experiences with the spiritual phenomenon, which I recall easily, happened sometime in 1986 in my rented bungalow, somewhere in Lagos. I saw a male figure in white standing on the air near the door do my bedroom closet some distance from the floor. He was in white glowing garment from neck to toe; only his head was uncovered, he was Caucasian. There was a glow of light around him from head to toe. He didn't say a word, only looked at me without any expression. I wasn't sleeping but was just about to go to sleep, just lying on the bed. I waited for the figure to speak but he didn't say a word and gradually faded away. I got out of bed immediately and knelt down to pray. I assumed he had come to judge me of some wrong-doing, or to warn me of some danger; and so asked God for forgiveness and protection. I was sober in spirit for weeks, wanted to tell someone but could not because I knew no one would believe me. Furthermore I felt I was so guilty that I didn't want to share my guilty complex with anyone. I gradually put the matter out of my mind, and didn't think much of it again until the strange experiences I began to have as described in this book. Had an angel come to warn me of danger?

My other experience happened in 1978. I was invited by a respected professional colleague to attend the Full Gospel Business Men's Fellowship International of Apapa, a maritime suburb on Lagos mainland on October 12, 1991. I still have the old invitation card which I wrote on, and had treasured ever since. This was the only paper I had to write with. Halfway through the prayer meeting session, a voice said in my hearing, as if sitting next to me, to stand up and sing a particular song. Being my first time at such a meeting, I started arguing internally with the voice and giving reasons why it would look odd for me, a total stranger and invited guest, to do that. This went on for a few seconds or minutes, and before I could give the rest of the reasons I was listing in my mind, another person stood up and started singing the same song the Holy Spirit had asked me to sing. I was shocked, and realized who I was dealing with and how I should have obeyed without question.

Immediately, I asked for forgiveness from God, then stood up and joined the man in the song until the end of the song; and didn't care anymore if anyone saw me or thought it odd. You know what, no one did. I knew that the day was significant and so was alert to receive subsequent spiritual directives, which I wrote down this time without questioning. These incidents shook me a lot and I also knew I was at that event for a purpose. So I sat down quietly at the end of our song and waited for the Holy Spirit. It came in the form of Glory be to God! Glory be to God! Glory be to God! I was to start a prayer Group meeting with some listed known people every Saturday 9a.m. This was for the well-being and safety of our husbands and children. I didn't hesitate to do as instructed, but explained to the team how I came to be inviting them. I kept the list still till today. I did as instructed and did not ask why. Usually one cannot fully know the reasons why spiritual instructions are given. Answers may come immediately or in stages or years after. Ours is to obey without question. However all we need do is to test the spirit and know that it is of God.

STAYING FOCUSED

Avoid deliberate distractions aimed at destabilizing you. Just as is done in battle strategy, there will be tactics used to distract, you, to confuse you and to derail your steps. Your one goal is to cling to God and never let Him go, morning, noon, and night. People who are not in your war may poke fun at you, call you names, cheat and lie against you, do all manner of injustice to provoke you. Never give in. The more they do these things the tighter, and the more you must cling to God, and never let Him go. Stay focused and don't fall for the tactics. Sometimes we too are tested by the Spirit to access our devotion, our faith, and our seriousness. Stay with God always, even if it looks as if He has ignored you. Stay with Him, your eyes on the ball. You remember that persistence pays all the time. Don't give up. At other times when temptations come to us, we must remain strong, thinking of the ultimate goal that we seek. Remember if you had come this far, you can hold on just long enough to complete the journey successfully. At such times, when I listened to the Pastors and Priests preach, I become encouraged and embolden to continue the good fight. I had often wondered if others go through these types of spiritual challenges. Preachers say yes, at one time or the other.

At such times, when I read the word of David in Psalm 71:1-24, I become renewed and strengthened.

TRIUMPHANT CONCLUSION

Even as I write this book, the ideas to express, the content to include, the passages to refer to, the structures to re-write, as well as the specific personal examples I included, all inspirations came as I wrote along, confirming the work of the Holy Spirit is forever, in all human endeavor. Finish the journey with the covenant of God to us in Isaiah 44:3 and on that covenant rest all our struggles, knowing it will be well and as He said, *"I am with you."* When God is with us, we have peace, victory, joy, and absolute satisfaction that it is well with us and ours. When God is with us, who can be against us? *"The grass withers, the flower fades, the word of God stands for ever"* Isaiah 40:8. *"God is our refuge and strength, a very present help in trouble"* Psalm 46:1. His covenant of protection, favor, blessings, victory, beauty, joy, peace and love for us, given us in His words will stand for a thousand generations. Psalm105:8. The Apostle Paul spoke often about God's peace, which passes all understanding; Gods peace in our lives and he sent peace to all the nations to which he wrote his apostolic messages. I also leave you God's peace for now and always.

CHAPTER 6

THE BLESSED VIRGIN MARY

INTRODUCTION

Every time and everywhere I see or read or hear the stories of the Blessed Virgin Mary, I am still fascinated by her life and work. In our house my family knows that I would sit and watch for hours stories of the life and times of the holy family every time they are on air.

The stories about her Apparitions fascinate me extremely. They were the first cases which showed to me the powers of the divine Father. All the messages and predictions she delivered from heaven to the world about world peace, global changes, and worship. She also brought sorrowful messages about world pain, deaths, and sins at which times she would weep real tears for humanity. South East Asia had some amazing apparitions of the Blessed Mother, so did South America, Mediterranean Europe, Eastern Europe and Africa. She came with major predictions for world peace and well-being. She advised mankind where to go, how to go when to go. All these are evidences of a faithful Mother of the world. I remain most enthralled by the Vision at Guadalupe and her divine messages to mankind.

I feel much honored indeed that she actually appeared to me in a dream to advise me of the solution to my predicament. In most of these appearances she preferred to appear as the Holy Immaculate Conception, one of her most revered images. Ever since our childhood, I recall that in our house, we have always had a picture of our mother Mary standing on the reptile snake. The picture must be over sixty years old. I have kept this picture most carefully with me up till now. She had truly watched over my family and had never left us, even though none of us ever bothered much with the picture I speak of now. It remained an important feature in our home. I am not sure where my parents got the picture from, but we still have it carefully placed over our home. Over the years it had remained the invisible, silent protector over us.

MY EXPERIENCES

The Holy Immaculate Conception truly continues to work miracles in the lives of her children. One day Ms. ABCD had come to my house apparently from church and a long drive to my place on her way to her house. She claimed she was very tired and wanted to rest in my bedroom. Like a sheep I led her to the room but stayed for a brief moment with her while she pretended to nap. After a while I left the room but kept the door opened, to go to the kitchen. About fifteen minutes later she came out saying she was rested and felt better. I thought the nap was unusually short and realized she was not in my room to nap, but to do something she didn't want me to see. She came into the parlor and again asked to rest on the couch on which I had been lying down to rest. At this time, I knew she was up to some mischief and left her to her wiles. She left after about ten minutes. Immediately, I went into the bedroom to bless it with holy water, I came out to bless by entire house with holy water and prayers. What this lady also didn't know was that the picture of the Blessed Virgin Mary I referred to above, rested on a wall and overlooked my entire bedroom, protecting the house where she rested. I would have sworn that the motherly image smiled at me as I sprinkled holy water round the bed and the house. Knowing she was looking over and after our home and all who lived in the house gave us much comfort and continues to give much needed assurances against the evil in the world.

WHAT THE HOLY BIBLE SAYS

As the Blessed Virgin Mary, mother, advocate and friend, her sufferings throughout her life and the life of her son Jesus Christ are well documented in the Holy Bible; from her betrothal through her pregnancy, during the early life of Jesus, through his passion, and at his death. She suffered a great deal. It was this that prompted me to seek her intervention for the then unexplained suffering I went through but could not stop or control. It was definite that I was up against strong powers and principalities. All who have the opportunity and those who don't have should create the opportunity to say and use the Holy Rosary to her honor, praying to God the Father, Son and Holy Spirit through her divine intercession. When a person is in crisis, what does the person have to lose? Use all opportunities to find succor, relief and solution. Call on Mother Mary, she always responds to those in need of her help.

DIVINE VESSEL & MOTHER

As the divine vessel, she quietly accepted the mission to bear the son of God at the Annunciation, knowing immediately what she would face in that era—the condemning looks, the hateful glances, the gossip, the evil whispers, the unguarded judgments, the rumors, the pain she would suffer, even possible death by stoning, all flashed before her eyes in the second she accepted the mission. But for the timely intervention of the Angel who appeared subsequently to Joseph, many were preparing the stones with which they planned to stone her to death. Nothing has changed since then. By the time the facts and the truth are known and these prove contrary to previous assertions, such people also lack the decency to seek forgiveness or apologizing to the wronged party. They usually move on to the next soul. I wonder if anyone went back to Mother Mary and asked God or her for forgiveness.

It is a great credit to her that though relatively young, she successfully weathered all storm, brought up Our Lord Jesus Christ and prepared him for His divine mission and ministry. She suffered in silence and emerged victorious to the whole world. God teach me to be patient and longsuffering. I have not been as our Blessed Mother was, in my trials.

PRAYING MOTHER MARY

Every woman, every mother whether biological mother or adoptive mother, must copy mother Mary and pray continually for our children, who are certainly inexperienced, innocent, and trusting, never imagining such evil abound around them, whether at home, in the neighborhood, in schools, and in fact, everywhere. Dear mothers, pray always for your children and without ceasing, just like Mother Mary.

Passionate Intercessor—She has always been an intercessor for us all with her son, and with God. She is the most arduous intercessor. She interceded for the wedding family at Canaan quite successfully. She knows the heart of her son best and has his love and ear.

The Holy Rosary is her specialty, enabling us to speak with her and gaining her confidence. When I went to speak with my Parish Priest in the years 2007 and 2008 when the satanic crisis was nearly drowning me, one of his suggestions was to say the Holy Rosary daily. I used to say the Holy Rosary once or twice a week before that time. Now, I say the Rosary daily; so much so that our Blessed Mother now knows me by name and not just that she knew my challenges, weaknesses, problems and warfare afflictions. Like a Mother-In-Israel, she took over my battle, called on her son to engage my enemies and the battle became won. Even now some of these groups of people who are still around don't realize that the power they face in the warfare was that of God, Father, Son, Holy Spirit and Mother Mary. They don't stand any chance. I am still in awe when I recall that she actually spoke with me as I recalled somewhere else in this book.

She had also interceded for nations and acted as the Divine Messenger. Often her messages have changed the course of history, of politics, of nations, of the Church of Christ on earth, of cultures, and indeed of the entire humanity. Furthermore, she still has not finished with us. She is still at work, with the Father and with her son Jesus Christ. Ironically, long before the age of Women's emancipation, God had chosen her for her maternal eternal role in heaven and on earth. Thank you Blessed Mother.

COUNSELOR & GENTLE WARRIOR

At Fatimah (Portugal), her messages were of divine counsel to the Church, and the World. These occurred on the thirteenth day of six consecutive months in 1917, starting on May 13. The three children were *Lúcia dos Santos* and her cousins *Jacinta and Francisco Marto.* Even then it took much disbelief, pain and suffering for her messages to become accepted. Some have interpreted her messages and appearances as being a "Change Agent" introducing the then unthinkable ideas of change into human history. In spite of the initial doubts, and even reluctance, change truly came.

At Lourdes (France), she appeared in the apparition of February 11, 1858, when *Saint Bernadette Soubirous*, a fourteen-year-old peasant girl who admitted to her mother that a "lady" spoke to her in the cave of Massabielle, (a mile from the town) while gathering firewood with her sister and a friend; to give divine prophecies and counsel to the Church and the world, to heal our spiritual and physical pains, illnesses, and inadequacies. This happened against initial church and political opposition and much suffering by the children.

At Guadalupe (Mexico) tradition relates that in the Sixteenth Century, on December 9, 1531, *Juan Diego*, a recently-converted *indigenous* Aztec *peasant*, had a vision of a young woman, a lady, while on a hill in the *Tepeyac* desert, near *Mexico City*. On this occasion, our Blessed Mother advocated the end to the sacrifices of children to gods though with gentle conviction, conversion of the natives and sustaining the gentle campaign for life even till today.

Over and over in this write up, I have described my dreams experiences and their eventual confirmations. The most impactful was the dream during the night between Saturday, January 9, 2010 to Sunday, January 10, 2010, when the holy Mother Mary appeared to me in a dream, and told me what to do to end the series of demonic oppression afflicting me. On that Saturday between 4p.m. and 5.30 p.m., I had gone to the Shrine of the Sacred Heart, 3211 Sacred Heart Way off 16th Street, in N.W. Washington, D.C. to seek her help to save me from the decade long torment by unknown, unseen forces. The subsequent dream remained a profound dream in answer to my earnest prayers.

MOTHER MARY'S CONCERNS FOR US

Mother Mary had sustained the world's children whom she considers her own children. She sought after our welfare and salvation. She also focused on mothers and motherhood, urging/encouraging us all to emulate her exemplary skills in prayerfully raising her son for his divine mission. She showed great concern for wars and their devastating effects on world peace and harmony. If we consider all of her interest carefully, we will see that the lives of children, mothers and their mothering roles are intricately interwoven, and are both affected usually adversely, by wars. When we consider that these have been among her key concerns over these past centuries, these indicate to us that we are still a long way to the true destination. Throughout all her earthly appearances, she also left us with several covenants and promises to help us through the earthly journey. She knew the dangers we would face, or are facing and she was there ready to hold our hands. Unfortunately, many Christians do not really know her or her immense powers for our earthly protection against evil. More of us should honor her and eulogize her accomplishments on earth and for mankind. Only few churches worldwide actually acknowledge her place in our lives; these are the Eastern Christian churches, the African Christian churches, and the global Catholic Church.

A PRAYER TO MOTHER MARY

"Mother Mary, blessed mother of our Lord Jesus Christ and a woman of favor with God, we ask you to place our request before the Throne of Grace, so that God may give more people more divine strength to work to eradicate the oppressive power of Satan, and make the world a better place. Kindly ask the Father to inspire and strengthen the people so that they might work to expose, fight and destroy satanic, demonic and witchcraft powers on earth. Help us to clean the world we live in of these evil influences so that the coming generations would have a better world in which to worship the Father. Amen."

---- ◄ CHAPTER 7 ►꜠----

LIVING IN THE SPIRIT

INTRODUCTION

Simply defined, Living in the Spirit means a life filled, controlled, experienced in the Holy Spirit, filled by the divine and directed by Godly pursuits, uncluttered by distractions of the world; A life which is striving for divine righteousness and purity. *2 Corinthians 5:17 "Therefore if anyone is in Christ, he is a new creation; old things have passed away; behold all things have become new."*

MY EXPERIENCES

When one dwells on, focuses on, or is constantly thinking about worldly matters, possessions, activities, issues, stories, conversations, challenges, problems, discussions, negative thinking, worldly activities-without-end, and a negative influence in the world etc., this tends to obstruct spiritual experiences. In the same way, continuous life of sin also detracts from experiencing the peace, joy and harmony which comes from a life in the spirit. Sin here refers to offenses against God's laws, or the law of nature. By contrast, a life in the spirit focuses on divine matters, activities, experiences, historical, biblical conversation, narrations, discussions, prayers, pursuit of all righteousness, praise, worship, thanksgiving, reflection in quiet moments, positive thinking, activities which encourage others, heal, inspire, promote, and enhance life, in short a positive influence or agent in the world. When I looked back over my life, I was the poster child of living in the world. However, and if the truth be spoken, I was constantly dissatisfied and seeking something fulfilling. I looked for succor with friends, with colleagues, with civic activities. I have since found out I was looking for meaning in the wrong places. The more I clung to these things, the more they slipped from my grasp. At this point I became sure that evil power was struggling to isolate me from the world and people around me. The more isolated I was, the more I clung to friends and people around me; and the harder also I tried to reconcile with anyone who might have had a conflict with me. I was very uncomfortable in any conflict with anyone at that time. Somehow, I needed people to hold on to so as to support me. Strangely, and one by one, an argument, disagreements, sudden conflicts, quarrels, and sometimes minor issues would become major fractions. One by one I became more and more isolated. At a stage, I decided to stop holding onto people, to let them go if they wished to leave me. On one occasion, one of my former friends was scolding me for a business matter after an argument. I was so tired of fights, and to stop this person from further words with me, I actually knelt down to beg her to stop. In the African culture, this gesture is the height of submission. Earlier, at a wedding ceremony, I had met an old gentleman whom I knew had ill feelings towards me; and also knelt down in public begging his forgiveness and understanding for the situation, but which had upset him. That was how decimated I had become. Rather than improve the matter, it got worse. So I accepted the end of all past relationships and acquaintances and moved forward in confidence that God would take care of me. It is true that demonic attacks tend to isolate the target from people in order to destroy that target. This is the outward physical effect of the spiritual imprisonment I was placed in, and which I discussed elsewhere in this book. However, I realized again that this isolation was un-natural and being instigated by external forces, although proving this in the normal world would be impossible. It just was too bizarre. The Lord God said I was not a victim, but a victor. I was destined to serve the Lord in the ways He had decided. No evil power can keep me imprisoned spiritually. So God used this situation to my advantage, using this isolation to take me from the world in which I had lived, so much so that I would focus only on Him, and His mission for me. At first, this was strange and difficult for me, but later when I understood what was happening to me, I simply accepted the Lord's will.

It was much later in 2009 that I understood how and why I was being isolated. In our lives' journeys we meet people and separate from people to follow our respective paths in life. In my own life's journey, the Lord said those who have departed from me for whatever reasons were not part of my future or I in their future. This only means that our lives' paths must separate at this point as we pursue God's design for us all. Also, I must walk alone from this stage on except with the Lord, in the process to fulfill the divine mission and purpose for my life. Therefore, I needed to be separated from most past contacts.

When I learnt this during one of teachings of the southern charismatic Preacher, I understood what was happening to me better, and so I stopped trying to hold on to former friends, family, and acquaintances that departed. I simply accepted their departures. I had to let go so I can be totally opened to follow my destiny. *"But now thus says the Lord who created you, O Jacob; And He who formed you O Israel. Fear not, for I have redeemed you; I have called you by your name. You are mine."* Isaiah 43:1

WHAT THE HOLY BIBLE SAYS

A person is totally blind when not living in the spirit. We know the Holy Spirit as a Tell-tale, Revealer of secrets, and an Inspiration. He gives knowledge where there is none; He confers wisdom where none exists; He opens the senses where these are dead; He shows us secrets we needed to see. A person who lives in the spirit also lives in God and God lives in him. When that happens, the person enters into an exceptional divine relationship. One can receive messages; one can hear warnings or cautions. One sees through dreams events around you. I didn't know this for a long time. When I was much younger, I usually experienced 'deja-vu' as I said elsewhere in this write up. They were actually dream visions which I had experienced before the event. Even during my study of Psychology, the definition of the concept was somehow different from what I now know it to be. I would stand someday and relive an entire event, a whole scene would play out before me, people who walked by, voices who spoke next, a laughter, a car sound, a bird that flew past, even my own comments or feelings at that time; I would relive the whole experience as in the same scene I had seen before. I now realize that I must have seen these scenes in a dream *before* I came to experience it again in waking life. I have had such experiences over and over again but didn't understand the significance. Now I do. After a while, I didn't have these visions again, I guess I was too much into the world. God forgive me. *1 Corinthians15:44 ". . . . There is a natural body; there is a spiritual body."* It distinguishes between Adam the man of flesh who was of the earth and full of corruption and who will return to dust; and Jesus Christ the Lord who came from heaven, the other man of the Spirit, who returned to heaven, without corruption.

The Holy Spirit chooses whom he would reveal himself to, whom He would open their eyes, increase their knowledge, and heighten their senses. He gives us different kinds of gifts to discern Him or His presence around us. Some see visions, some hear messages, and some have the spirit of understanding. Some people dream dreams just as Joseph the dreamer in the Bible, some have the power to lay hands on in healing, others to pray, others still have the gift to love, serve, and share. The spirit is manifested in truly different ways in mankind. The Apostle Paul was a shining example of a person living in the spirit. Throughout his writings, during his travels, teachings, and during his imprisonment, he exemplified the man in whom the Holy Spirit lived. That was why virtually all his Letters to nations reflected the Living Holy Spirit in him. In Romans 8:2, he spoke of himself *"For the law of the Spirit of life in Christ Jesus has made me free from the law of sin and death."* He also described how it is to live in the Spirit. *"For those who live according to the flesh set their minds on the things of the flesh, but those who live according to the Spirit, the things of the spirit. For to be carnally minded is death, but to be spiritually minded is life and peace."* Romans 8: 5&6. *"But you are not in the flesh but in the Spirit. If indeed the Spirit of God dwells in you. Now if anyone does not have the Spirit of Christ, he is not His."* Romans 8:9. He gave us further examples of what the Spirit does in our lives. *"Likewise the Spirit also helps in our weaknesses. For we do not know what we should pray for as we ought, but the Spirit Himself makes intercession for us with groaning which cannot be uttered."* Romans 8:26.

When we face demonic dangers, Paul assures us that the Holy Spirit supports and defends us in battle. *"For you did not receive the spirit of bondage again to fear, but you received the Spirit of adoption by whom we cry out Abba, Father. The Spirit Himself bears witness with our spirit that we are children of God." Romans 8:15-16.*

On one occasion during the period I was living in fear, I knew I was under some form of evil power, but I didn't know who or where or why or when of the situation. Who would I turn to for help, there was no one able to see or understand my situation. I was also afraid to tell anyone the full extent of what I was going through, for fear I would be labeled negatively. On a few occasions I tried to tell some people around me who had shown some sort of concern for my tension and somewhat agitated occasional complaints to them; I didn't do a good job of it as even I couldn't articulate clearly what I was going through. I was in constant fear and anxiety because I didn't know what was happening to me, except that I was under a siege of sorts. The voice of the Holy Spirit calmed me clearly one evening by quoting a Bible passage which I had heard, written down somewhere but forgotten at that time. *2 Timothy 1:7 said "For God has not given us a spirit of fear, but of power and of love and of a sound mind."* I was elated and knew again that the Spirit of God was fighting for me. He just strengthened me by the passage quoted. From then on I stopped being afraid and I became emboldened, knowing that I too can do all things through Christ who strengthens me. I have not looked back since. I have marched forward from victory unto victory in God the Father, in Jesus Christ the Son and in the Holy Spirit.

CONCEPTS OF LIVING

I used to wonder what it was to live. Is it a Philosophical inquiry? Is it a Biological question? Is it a Sociological question? Is it a Spiritual phenomenon? I suppose it is a bit of all these and maybe more. Growing up we were raised to go to school, gain good education, that usually meant going through some higher education so as to earn a living income to sustain oneself; learn housework so that when one became a wife and mother, the basics of domestic science would have been learned; get married, have children and go to church on Sundays; attend family and friends parties, take vacations, make some good investments, have some harmless fun and grow old in dignity. Do some good deeds; belong to Church societies, social groups and societies in order to belong. I did all these things and was never truly happy. I also learned early in life that unhappiness was an acceptable part of life. So one accepted some disappointments, some pain, some unattained dreams, some tears along with blessings from the Lord. Some people seemed to have the good things of life virtually handed over to them; some others seemed to struggle for things in life. I was one of those who found me struggling for every little possession, every little success, and every occasional joy. A few times I would sit back and wonder why my life seemed so difficult compared to others around me. After a series of prayers for God to change my life to be easier, He would reply me in a particular song in the Yoruba language. This was a favorite song which I received over and over again. *"S'ise ninu ogba Oluwa re . . . . Wa s'ise ki 'kore to de"* translated, *'Work in the garden of your God . . . . You must work before your harvest comes."* This message was unmistakable. At first it didn't strike me in any way, but when it was repeated to me over and over again, and at every turn of my life, I sat up and took notice. So I tried to work in His garden by doing good deeds where ever I saw someone in need. Whenever I saw a need in an Institution, in Charity organizations, in any area of life where there was an opportunity to give, I gave and tried to work as directed. I was unstoppable. Apparently, this was just the initial training for the work which the Lord God had in mind for me. *To live is to serve God with our being, talents and strengths.* By this time I had come to know through the revelation of the Holy Spirit the work which God had assigned me as my destiny to serve Him. *All the demonic battles He had allowed me to experience, which He had fought for me and overcame, and the accompanying divine victories He gave me, were part of the training experience to know His voice, see His power, understand His will, and instructions to me.* All around me, those powerful entities that rose up against me were vanquished like flies; one after another. These people were confronting the mighty power of God Almighty. I soon realized this quickly and was full of awe for the power of God. Some people around me also saw these mighty shows of God's power, but most assumed that I must have some unusual powers, somehow. There is no going back. I no longer belong to myself and must walk very carefully in the strict path designed for me by God. In 2009, during a brief visit to Nigeria, I was attending a church service at the Laughter Foundation Cathedral Church in Lagos, when during the sermon the Prophet of God and Pastor, stopped briefly after his teachings and said *"There is a woman here who had been facing serious demonic battles. It is God who had been fighting for you. Never think that the victories are by your own praying powers only.*" I noted this message in my small notebook, but I already knew without doubt, that he was referring to me. It was also in that church that God delivered His covenant of total protection for me, retribution against all who had fought satanic battles with me, and the promise to reveal Himself to the world as my Savior, in *Isaiah 49:25& 26*, and in another pronouncement by the Pastor, while I was in the church on another occasion. Everyone who is reading my story, and who is suffering under the bondage of witchcraft or other demonic affliction, should know that only the person who approaches God personally can receive grace for salvation and deliverance. One of the first steps to take is to submit to God totally. James 4:7-8 says "*Therefore submit to God, resist the devil and he will flee from you. Draw near to God and He will draw near to you. Cleanse your hands, you sinners; and purify your hearts, you double minded.*" This is a clear and simple divine instruction.

A LIFE IN THE FLESH

In Romans chapters five through to chapter eight, the blessed Apostle Paul describes what it is to live a life of the flesh. As I studied the passages, I concluded that it was profound reading. A life in the flesh is one of sinfulness, acts against the commandments of God, a life of ungodly behavior and ungodly conduct, a life of certain death, a life of unrighteousness, a life destined for divine judgment. It is only by the grace of God we are able to truly live a life in the Spirit. A lot of things became clearer to me as I went on the journey; and I realized that I am not the same person I was some years ago. I have also heard a popular television Preacher talk about how the world would fight a person in transformation, how even some established churches of Christians, or other Christians would fight against the person, push the person out or isolate him/her even if left in their midst. He reminded listeners how Christ was also isolated, rejected and ostracized in His days by the establishment religious people. According to him, the servants of God would also be treated in a similar manner. He said throughout the history of Christianity various servants of God on Godly missions were similarly abused and isolated. This was quite amazing to me because a few months earlier the Holy Spirit had warned me to expect to serve

God alone, that people around me would reject me, isolate me and ostracize me, for a while; and that when the time comes, He would bring new contacts, new people and new support into my life, that I need not be alarmed when I see these happening. Very soon after, I did see this isolation happen, but didn't mind at all, because it became the manifestation of the prophecy I had received. I was in the world in a big way; however I went through a transition from a life in the flesh, to a life in the Spirit because I was being prepared to serve God in a way not then imagined, but which he had destined me for.

WORLDLY ATTRACTIONS

The glittering world of power, fame, money, gold or other precious metals, possessions, clothes, popularity, sex, alcohol, drugs, food, government taxes, and bills are among the usual elements which constitute our focus on earth. If we are not chasing something, something is chasing us. The tension in the world and the dissatisfaction we all face are results from these attractions. We have continued to see one economic depression and another, sliding into major recessions in virtually all parts of the world. More and more people become poorer, more hungry, sick, homeless, and helpless. It is almost as if the more we strive to get them, the more tension, dissatisfaction we experience. We are in constant struggle against one economic crises or another, against political dictatorships and oppressions of the masses, whether disguised or undisguised. There is so much dissatisfaction with our human lives; some cultures say that life in this world is akin to sorrows and pain. Christians eagerly look forward to the 'life to come', the life in heaven. There is always something missing, a void difficult to fill with worldly goods. It is only when our life is God-filled do we experience true satisfaction, joy, and contentment; yet God is Spirit, and therefore His life in us is spiritual. No wonder the Holy Bible says "Seek ye first the Kingdom of God and all other things shall be added unto you." I have often sat down in utter wonder listening to people who have had near death experiences recount their heavenly experiences. One of the things they often shared was their feeling of joy, peace and contentment, and a reluctance to depart from the presence of holiness such as they had, to return to the earth. All over the world, from the East to the West, from the North to the South, ancient wisdom had demonstrated that there is a world of goodness outside this life, there is a higher kind of existence beyond our earthly understanding. Perhaps we all should be better off striving for this higher life than the constant struggles we face here on earth. The Holy Bible advises us to store up treasures for ourselves in heaven, not on earth. The earthly possessions rot, or are stolen or vanish and certainly don't last. Ask some people who have made money but suddenly find they have become totally penniless. Ask politicians who have suddenly lost power and positions, and have had to adjust back to life as ordinary citizens, lucky that they had not lost their lives in the reversal. I admit that at some time in my past, I have also traditionally enjoyed some worldly goodies. Recently between year 2009 to early 2011 when I became constantly worried about getting a better more permanent job, worried about my rent, about my health and health insurance, about bills, and everything related to life; the Holy Spirit advised me to focus less on worldly matters and instead focus more on heavenly matters. He promised to 'take care of me.' In an amazing way which I quite can't explain, I have not lacked for anything since I left my care entirely to God.

FOCUS ON HEAVEN

A heavenly focus is a total life lived solely for the life to come in heaven. All the Apparitions of the Blessed Virgin Mary on earth during her memorable visits to the earth have convinced all humanity that heaven is real and the only focus we should aspire to. A focus on heaven reflects in those who are taking every step with the thought of heaven in mind. When one hears some of the stories of 'near death' experiences recounted by different individuals, males, females, and children who went through these experiences, one will be affected positively. There are also cases of other people who have had real visions of heaven. There are other cases where others have experienced the pain and devastation of hell that when they were given another chance at life, they had reformed completely. There are several unexplained phenomenon which ordinary human capability cannot explain to us. Surely there is a super-human power recognizable in these experiences. How can anyone explain the phenomenon of Stigmatisms? Science has proved incapable to explain this phenomenon experienced by certain holy people, who bear the same bodily marks as Jesus Christ at his passion; and often during the celebration of that Passion of Christ, or at other special occasions, and who would shed blood just as Christ did during His earthly passion. Exceptional miracles have occurred all over the world which could only be results of heavenly interventions in human lives; so are many other miraculous healing, unexplained recoveries not attributable to sudden healing syndrome. If one explores the concept closely, there is no such thing as Sudden Healing Syndrome or whatever name is attached to this phenomenon. An unseen divine intervention happened to change the state from deceased to good health. These are cases we must keep in constant mind while we live. They are enough for wise people to seek and focus on heaven, not just as a solution against earthly pain, but a worthwhile destination to seek after, as a primary goal.

PERSONAL TRANSFORMATION

A recent teaching by a television Preacher, advocates in us all a total transformation in spirit, in behavior, in perception, in orientation and focus. This is a rebirth from the inside out, so much so that the new being is totally different from the former person. The respected Bishop and Pastor recently also explained why God takes individuals through personal changes. According to him, God puts a person in certain situations of fire, severe social discomfort, frustrations in one's environment, and sometimes isolated for one's own development. At other times divine change is forced on the person by irritating circumstances in one's current life and lifestyle in order to bring about desired change, as one grows from one spiritual level into another. Although the eventual new life is a rewarding existence, the person in transformation may not immediately appreciate or enjoy the process of the change. The southern charismatic Preacher likened the process of transformation to the maturing of a pearl from the irritation of sand in the oyster, or the formation of steel going through the blast furnace and emerging into the perfect metal. Others have also likened this change to the formation of diamond when coal goes through intense heat. 'No pain, no gain'. In short, the change process which results in the new person is almost always painful, uncomfortable and heated. Our consolation is that we have God's promise to give to us only as much as we can withstand, and His assurance of His presence with us in all situations. At one stage or another, life itself takes people through 'Change', whether for good or for not-so-good, shocking or tranquil.

At the end of such experiences the person emerges as different whether or not the changes are visible to others; a change had certainly taken place.

"Oh God in heaven touch our lives and transform us to be instruments of service to you on earth; use us to touch lives positively, to make the world a better place and to fight evil with prayers. Surround us with your grace, to do your will always, make us good examples of Your Spirit in man and take us wherever you will. Amen."

$\dashv$ CHAPTER 8 $\vdash$

DIVINE COMMUNICATIONS

INTRODUCTION

The usual concept of Communication, as a human behavior and experience also exists in divine or spiritual communications. My experiences, described previously tell me without doubt that the Holy Spirit delivers the voice of God to man. This happens through our senses, through our physical bodies, through other people, through animals, through the elements, through pictures, and art forms which cry, shed tears or present unusual phenomena to us, through space and time. God can use anything to communicate with us.

WHAT THE HOLY BIBLE SAYS

The word of God stands forever. The word of God is life. The word of God is truly alive. The word of God goes out to fulfill the divine wish, never to return void. "Because He has said so, it is fulfilled; because he has commanded it, is shall stand forever". The word of God is very precious, He speaks seldom, but when He does, hold it because it stands forever. His words cannot be forced. We have to wait patiently for Him, assured that our prayers are going up to Him. *Psalm 27:14 "Wait on the Lord; Be of good courage, and He shall strengthen your heart; wait, I say on the Lord."* For sure God the father, Son and Holy Spirit speak to us as it pleases. He speaks to us just as two people speak to each other. God speaks through intermediaries like Priests, Pastors or ordinary people. There is no one that cannot be used by God to pass His communications. God speaks to us through dreams, through visions, other non-verbal methods, He speaks to us through a medium usually space, through our spirit realm, or through our physical senses. He warns us of danger. He gives us reassurances when we are afraid. He gives us covenants of victory or wellbeing throughout life. He offers gifts of love, victory, salvation, peace, honor, favor, blessings, joy, contentment, and strength to us.

DIVINE MESSENGERS

The Blessed Virgin Mary is the most favorite divine messenger or communicator through whom God had often spoken to the world. She had brought these messages at strategic periods in human history. Her messages are direct from God. At other times God had sent angels, Cherubim and Seraphim, to deliver His messages in human voices. There are times when God would decide to speak to us directly. We could never know why He chooses one method one medium or another. He is God. Virtually every one of the divine intervention recalled in this book were examples of divine messages alerting us to danger, assuring us of His power to save, taking over our battles, directing our paths in the right direction or calming our fears by His presence in us or around us.

PRAYER

Our prayer is the language of communication to God, in whichever dialect we wish to speak. He founded speech and so understands all human, animal, and divine languages. In submission and total reverence, our standard prayers are usually in three parts; a period of Adoration and Worship; a portion of Thanksgiving; and a section for voicing the purpose of our communication. I now know that every prayer is received by God. In this case we must ensure total respect, devotion and honor during our prayers. We could even pray in quiet thoughts, vocalized or not. He may choose not to respond to us immediately, but there is always a response to all prayers. The feedback may come in unusual forms or in the usual forms listed above. The response may be pleasant, or unpleasant. Remember, when God admonishes us, it is for our own good, and because He loves us. When we pray, irrespective of whether or not we receive a reply, we must pray without ceasing. When we pray we are building up our divine bank account, confident that we would have a full account to draw on in the future. When we pray, we must open up to receive a reply which can come at any time. I have experienced every type of element described above here, in my journey with God.

SONGS & HYMNS

Songs and hymns are other ways in which we communicate with the divine God. As I had explained somewhere, He also responds to us through songs. Every time He had given me a song whether solicited or not by me, I knew there was a definite message, reply, advice, blessing, favor given to me in the particular song. We may sing off key, we may sing loudly, we may sing in low tones, we may just even hum songs in praise, worship, adoration or prayers, but sing we must. God also enjoys our voices raised to Him in prayer, praise and worship. I was almost over-sleeping my early morning prayer meeting with God one day, and apparently the hosts of heaven were all set and waiting for the discussion, when He woke me up with the song "Stand Up and Bless the Lord. The Lord your God adore . . . ." I was elated, jumped up and started our early morning discussion session. At other times, I would burst out singing a particular song rather involuntarily. At first since I wasn't paying attention to the message, I would hear a voice telling me to listen to the words of the song, then when I paid attention, I would realize that there were particular communication for me, a specific meaning at that period or moment, in the song I was singing. When this happened over and over again, I soon grew to realize that this is a direct communication for me. Now when I sing, I know that I am receiving a feedback or a new communication from God. At other times, when a Priest or a Preacher is preaching, at a particular point in the series, the voice would get me to pay attention to that portion of the lecture because it was very relevant for me. Surely many of us have also had these same experiences. It is a romantic and exhilarating experience.

LISTENING & FEEDBACK

We need to listen attentively to receive divine feedback in our communications with God. Our dreams and visions are significant and must never be discarded. Our role is to pay attention, actively and await the expected response. We are to be emotionally prepared to receive

His feedback. After prayers, it is a good practice to wait patiently for a few minutes, moments, and thereafter be conscious and expectant of feedback which could come in any form.

There are also many ways to 'Hearing the Spirit'. Sometimes, the experiences might seem strange to ordinary life, but there is nothing strange in the voice of God. The bible tells us not to harden our hearts, in order that we might experience Him. The feedback may come while we are asleep and we are woken up to hear the reply. It may come from a servant of God.

It was on April 16, 2008, just before I relocated to the US that I received a landmark feedback from God. The Prophet and Pastor of Laughter Foundation Cathedral delivered the message during a church service that "A lady here who had been pursued by dogs in her dreams for several years has been delivered by God." I was thrilled, and have since been full of joy and thanksgiving to God. The realities of God's powers are true and valid.

OUR DREAMS

Many years ago, I saw myself in a dream in the warehouse described elsewhere in this book. That warehouse had no door but some wired high windows from where some light streaked in, and from where I could hear voices from the outside. I tried but couldn't get out or escape. There were two dogs on guard who would growl at me or bark fiercely every time I tried to leave the room. In the dream I sensed danger and fear all around me. The Lord was showing me that I (in my spirit) was a captive and imprisoned although my physical body was living in the natural world. It was in this captive state that Ms. ABCD controlled my life, every key aspect of my normal life, mind control, giving me controlling instructions, monitoring my movements, interactions, relationships, and other activities; and easily intervening at will. She had decided I was to serve her and for a while she owned me, while appearing as a friend. In life she would drop hints of things she wanted me to do for her in different forms; and thinking I was being helpful would respond happily, indeed eager to support a person in need. The meaning of this dream was clear to me as a communication from God, so that I would know the seriousness of the situation I was in. I declared that God did not create me to serve any sorcerer, witch, wizard or demon. He created me to live a life full of divine purposes, and to honor Him, doing His will for creating me.

After a series of dedicated prayers, God delivered me. In a second similar dream I saw myself in that same warehouse prison, and suddenly a space opened in the wall with bright white lights streaming into the enclosure, the dogs were nowhere to be seen and I simply walked out into the outside world. Much later in 2006, God then pronounced His covenant of total eternal protection for me and of everlasting vengeance against my enemies throughout Isaiah 49: 1-26, but especially in verses 25 and 26; so that I, the former captive of the mighty was taken away, and I, the former prey of the terrible was delivered and freed forever.

In the same way and by the mighty right hand of God, every captive soul, every prey of terrible demonic forces, shall be freed as they read my story in this book and as they call on God to also deliver them.

Extra Sensory Perceptions ESP

The gift of Discernment enables the person to know things not easily known or available to others. Something in you just tells you what you need to know for your wellbeing, safety, goodness, and victory.

Vibrations—Although many people make fun of them, the power of God manifests in diverse ways as it pleases. People also have been given different forms of spiritual gifts depending on the assignment or purpose for which God requires of them. It is also through these special gifts that He speaks to and through His people. He still speaks in thunder, lightning, storms, and earthquakes. He speaks through the inspired Biblical speakers we see all around us.

Heat-The well-known thermal touch sensation is another medium of divine non-verbal speech. He communicates healing sometimes through thermal sensations.

ESP-There are many gifted individuals with extra sensory perception, and who are able to envision scenes distant from them, or at locations they were never present. Some are able to see ghosts walking around us; hear voices clearly either of angels, holy spirits, or even of evil spirits and of ghosts.

SPIRITUAL ALERTNESS

It is okay to be different. A person living in the spirit is a different person from others around. Furthermore, unless one is spiritually alert, one may miss the subtle communications of the Holy Spirit. A wise preacher said recently that that difference is seen by the adversarial Satan, who then mounts attacks against the person. We must be alert, always on our guard, through unstoppable and unending prayers. That's how to call on the grace of God in battle.

In response to prayers, I saw the power of God rise up in anger against those who tried to destroy me. He asked me to hold still and know that He is God. He told me to watch and see what He would do to all the demonic adversaries around me. As I said earlier, the war of tongues is used to multiply adversaries; in addition satanic members, though unknown to one, are invited to attack the subject in support of their kind. Indeed they were many, these deadly servants of Satan, whose only purposes in life are to steal, kill, and destroy the people of God. I didn't understand many behaviors around me because they seemed strange. However the Holy Spirit kept me asking the *Why* questions over and over, and by the grace of God, I started to see the whole picture of the fragmented pieces I saw initially. I urge readers also to ask God to show what things you need to see, what you need to hear, what you need to know, about your life, so that you can seek His powers to defeat satanic enemies. Our God is a righteous judge, deliverer of the oppressed, and savior of the person in bondage. *Psalm 48:10 says "According to your name O God, so is your praise to the ends of the earth. Your right hand is full of righteousness."*

The people of God should be aware, careful and sensitive, if it looks as if you are being isolated from your family, siblings, positive friends and business associates. Isolation from those usually around you is another way which witches attack the target. They can achieve their goal when that target is isolated and alone. In the midst of others, these others are able to see the negative changes going on in the life and behavior of the target. The satanic spirit may be the only person coming round to visit regularly, appearing to be a concerned friend.

⁓⊰ CHAPTER 9 ⊱⁓

EXISTENTIAL DANGERS

INTRODUCTION

My experiences are the main sources of my comments here. I am sure that these are very limited even as harrowing as they have been. I will try to describe the modus operandi of demonic agents as far as I saw these activities. Many Christians are like timid innocent lambs in the hands of these witches and wizards. These demonic agents would have received satanic powers usually through an older family member, or as a generational family inheritance, or through peer invitation, or they might have stumbled into the cult on their own willingly or by accident. These powers enable them to do evil things, unnatural manipulations, perform demonic activities, and terrorize the people of God. 'The innocence of the lambs' is an apt expression which describes how innocently they interact with these people. Demonic forces and witchcraft members operate in a network across continents and they recognize one another wherever they meet, in social events, gatherings, in businesses, in schools and even in churches. At the height of their evil, they call on demons to attack the soul and life of another person. They are relentless, know no family or friends. All who are not with them is an enemy, a foe to be destroyed. They offer support to their kind in battle and warfare. They will do all they could to avoid detection or exposure.

WHAT THE HOLY BIBLE SAYS

It is no wonder that the Holy Bible say we should pray without ceasing, for we are in constant battle. We are to put on the armor of righteousness, the chalice of valor and the shield of justice. The greatest danger is that of idol worshipping. This separates the person from the love of God. The Holy Bible tells us over and over again that God is a jealous God. He will not share His people with mere idols, the handwork of mere men. The demonic powers struggle daily to win over the people of God to their membership. They torment an innocent person, oppress him or her through something dear to the person and then entice him or her into their cult in order to 'belong'. The Holy Bible warns us to beware. They are all offspring of Jezebel, who was very powerful and a priestess of Baal; she used her evil power to oppress, and mislead the people of God during the time of the prophets Elijah and Elisha, the servants of God. One of the reasons for the downfall of Solomon, was that he permitted idols to be erected and worshipped in Israel, even though by the foreign wives whom he had married for so-called political reasons. This was unacceptable corruption in the eyes of God. There are many positive uses of the mass media and of telecommunications in the current century. Unfortunately, they have also been used for many evil, harmful, unproductive and negative purposes. The passages in Proverbs, the messages of Isaiah and those of Jeremiah have many learning points for us, helping and guiding us through our world.

WHERE ARE THE DANGERS

Existential dangers are the pitfalls of routine life of ordinary people who may not know the dangers ahead. These include the following-

- Dangers of Lifestyle. Many people have been destroyed easily through lifestyle pitfalls in eating, drinking, indiscriminate sexual activities, drugs, gang membership, social gatherings, clubs and associations, peer groupings, schools, and other social institutions. Even the touch of witches on your body causes harm. That is why people avoid them like the plague, and that is why they hide their true identities among regular normal peoples. This habit of sharing or exchanging clothes is deadly, if not unhygienic.

- Dangers from Others. I have seen movies where friends invite their friends into witchcraft. I also was invited to join a 'white garment church'. On the third invitation as explained earlier in this book, I realized that I was being invited to join a witchcraft cult. By the fourth invitation, I made it clear to the sponsor, that I was not interested. Many public teachings of churches have warned people against accepting invitations to 'White garment churches' generally understood to mean an invitation to witchcraft. I wonder how many other women have been recruited into witchcraft in this way. I also understand that there are many truly Christian Churches who wear white garment as a religious tradition of worship. These are not to be confused with the satanic groups. The companies our children keep are sometimes deadly company. Our parents should be more spiritually alert, and daily cover their children with the blood of Jesus. Going to friends' homes to play, eat, and sleep, is a dangerous practice for our children. If the house embraced witchcraft, they could use one's garments and introduce demonic weapons into the clothes. Our churches also need to take urgent actions against these satanic recruitment strategies.

- Dangers to the Body. Some examples of such atrocities are unexplained illnesses; strange physical symptoms of bodily malfunction, not easily explained through medical diagnosis of pathologies; sudden deaths around the persons, chronic, and sustained attacks to the head in the form of headaches or migraines, not controlled by usual medications. A feeling of pin-prick in sensitive parts of the body like eyes. Witches have been known to take elements of menstrual periods to use in demonic rituals to destroy fertility. Only their members know the methods they use, but one has seen the effect of their actions.

- Dangers to the Soul. The most devastating attacks are against the human soul and spirit. They do this through isolation, through antagonistic reactions from others, through restlessness, through stress, and by creating anxiety, they have been known to destroy mental peace, and so create mental illnesses, paranoia, and outright schizophrenia in the lives of targets. This is the most deadly because the innocent medical practitioner would be treating mental illness, not fully understanding the cause of it. In any case he probably does not believe in the deadly effect of witchcraft, and so would assume other causes for the illness. The result is that the patient would never be cured.

- Dangers that attack the Spirit. A person or spirit under attack is perpetually in sorrow, constantly unhappy, facing unending paranoia, other behavioral disorders, and mental problems, but may be unable to articulate the problems. I was once in that mode, and unable to discuss with anyone. Half of the world does not even believe in witchcraft; there lies a factor for the huge success of witchcraft in the world; another half would assume the real problem is a psychological pathology. I used to attend a church where another woman I knew from our school days, was in perpetual state of unhappiness. Something bothered her all through the years I knew her. She looked always unhappy as if under a spiritual siege. She eventually died suddenly and mysteriously. It is unnatural to live in a state of near perpetual stress as she did.

- Dangers from Demonic forces. When the battle is difficult for the protagonist, or when they want to do deadly, devastating damage, they invite their demon into the battle and hand over the innocent lamb to the demon. Unless the person is living in the Spirit, the person would be dying on their feet without finding the cause of it. Normal prayers over the situation would require the specific and targeted intervention by God against the demon, for the person to be delivered. Remember I had been there as well. I am alive today only by the grace of God, Eli, and Jehovah the conqueror of evil; so that I could fulfill His divine assignment to write my story for the world to read. This story is not fiction.

- Danger to the body. The ensuing stress is physically debilitating. Being under immense internal turmoil, stress, and tension, I was grinding down my teeth in my sleep for several years. I didn't realize this physical change to my dentition, it was my Dentist who first called my attention to it, when she noticed the surfaces of my teeth were getting lower and lower. She explained the process, and that very stressful emotional problems of the patient could cause teeth grinding. I admitted I had been stressed for years, but didn't tell her more.

- Dangers from telecommunications. I understand that witches are able to send curses, witchcraft commands and evil incantations over the phone into the ears, head and spirit of the receiver through tactical pauses in the conversation. One of the books by Dr. D.K Olukoya described incidents of satanic use of technology and how to deal with such problems.

- They are known to change their bodily forms into various animals, dogs, cats and birds; even disguise their faces and take on other peoples' forms and faces, to carry our deadly activities. This enables them to hide their identity, and to throw suspicion on another party. They use animals such as wall geckos and lizards, to listen into conversations in one's homes, while they could be miles away. Be careful about Trojan gifts such as bracelets, beads, wrist watches, pendants, scarves, rings etc. Witches use these items to monitor the person 24/7, or introduce evil potions into the innocent through these objects, once the person wears the item.

- Sometime in January 2012, a relation who was staying with me couldn't find her wrist watch on the dressing table where she had left it the previous night. We searched everywhere in that room and then gave up. A week later the wrist watch was found neatly placed on a nearby packaging box. We threw the old watch away and thought it strange that the watch had disappeared for a week. Soon after, my pair of eye glasses which I normally leave on my bedside furniture, as I go to sleep disappeared one morning. Again I looked all over the bedroom, in all handbags, in corners around the house, under my bed, all over the entire house for the glasses for two weeks. I didn't understand what had happened to the glasses. Two weeks later, the eye glasses was returned and found neatly folded under my bed, and in a place where I had looked every day in the previous two weeks. Then it struck me; just as in the case of the wrist watch, something or someone took the eye glasses away for a short time for a purpose, perhaps the person wanted to be able to see what I was doing, where I was going, who I was talking to, through the glasses. Stranger than fiction but true; I never wore the glasses again but threw it away.

THE BODY/SOUL/SPIRIT/BEHAVIOR DIMENSION

When they attack the soul, their purpose is to destroy the spirit and the emotional well-being of the person. This attack is reflected in the physical bodily health or the unusual behavior of the person. This person is responding or reacting to what is only being experienced by him, as he is attacked by unseen forces. Perception is reality. His reactions are not necessarily a mental illness, but rather a response to that which only he is going through. He cannot even begin to explain to others what, or how, or why, or when he is being attacked. Others, who do not understand what he is going through, may categorize the external behavior as abnormal. The normalcy of his behavior is in the reality of his oppression by unseen demonic agents through secret methodologies, using the spiritual medium to transmit their deadly attacks.

When the person prays reverently to God, Father, Son and Holy Spirit, being just and righteous, and promising deliverance from such attacks as these; they then rise up also to counter the demonic attack to the soul, through the spirit, and resulting in a healthy well-being in the physical body, as well as in the normalcy of behavior. *Apart from the power of God, there is no other weapon against demonic attacks. Our human abilities are useless before these satanic agents. They operate in the spirit while we living in the physical flesh, are unable to access the spiritual dimension. They are strongest between midnight and up to about 3a.m., during which period various writings have told us they operate. This is* also the time when the spirit of a person is most vulnerable because the person is asleep, but in a subconscious state. The beauty of living in the Spirit is that even when asleep, the soul is active and can pray or sing or call on the divine, if faced with sudden danger in that sleep. Many people have been known to call on the name of Jesus, to pray or sing to God in their sleep. Others around them would only hear the prayer or the song, but would never imagine the reason for such sleep or subconscious vocalization.

Recall that the Apostle Paul had warned us of the enormous evil power of satanic and demonic forces. At the same time, he told us what to do to overcome them. No matter how strong they are, they are no match for Angelic warriors such as Holy Archangel Michael, whom the Father may send into battle on our behalf. These witches and demonic agents know our human incapacities very well, and so look at those people not in their cult with total but subdued contempt, toying with the lives of their oppressed as they please. The Holy Bible tells us that we do not need to suffer any kind of oppression if only we turn to the Divine Holy God, who is our sanctuary, our salvation, our strength, and our tower of protection. The beauty of our Godly victory is that these defeated evil agents cannot ever complain in public, or out loud of their defeat. They and all their types must suffer their defeat, and any judgment and punishment delivered to them by God. In this case, they have no one to appeal to. They are damned forever. *"God overcame the world and gave us victory." John 16:33.*

My Experiences

On Saturday, January 24, 2009, I was at home in the United States, planning to do some domestic work around the house when *I heard very clearly the Holy Spirit telling me to go immediately to the church where I normally attended Mass.* The voice was so clear and unmistakable, that I knew this was urgent. So I dropped all other plans and went to the church. I met a group who were spending the day at a special Prayer Retreat. So I joined them and prayed. At about 12 noon, we had a brief open period for private prayers, so I went into the Chapel to pray privately and to wait for the Lord. As soon as I finished praying, I heard the Holy Spirit again say *"Sanctuary! Sanctuary! Sanctuary! So I repeated this several times immediately for about twenty-one times.* I sat still for a few more seconds, thanked God for the battle He had just won for me and then left joyfully. I recalled the use of this statement in olden days when a person sought and obtained freedom from persecution, and from prosecution from some higher or greater power, once that person ran into the church for safety. I didn't have to know the what, where, who, when, or the whys of this event. I knew without doubt, that I needed to be in the house and presence of God at the particular time, when a terrible war was raging around me. God is awesome. I write these things as directed by the spirit even now so that the children of God need not suffer under any demonic oppression. If we all could see the hateful evil spirits, and demonic creatures with which we live daily, we would not need any Pastors or Priests to beg us to seek God. We would beg these holy servants of God to show us how to find God Almighty at all costs. Nothing we do on earth is more important than seeking God, holding fast unto His legs, and seeking His righteousness. I have learnt the hard way, going through forty-two years of demonic oppression, before I was delivered. During that period, it took me a long time to realize that my life was being forcibly controlled by negative forces outside my control. As a daily, weekly, monthly and yearly routine, every person should re-examine their lives, assess their situations, evaluate their lives' journeys, their relationships with God, their consciences, and their handworks; and effect necessary personal changes in their total lives, primarily for the kingdom of God. It is in doing this that all other needs, wants, and goals sought, would be added unto us.

⚔ CHAPTER 10 ⚔

THE CHURCHES' ROLES IN SPIRITUAL WARFARE

INTRODUCTION

Let me share more of my experiences with you for a moment. I got to a stage where I knew I was being manipulated by external forces beyond my natural strengths, yet I couldn't reach out for help for many years. I didn't know who to turn to. At a stage in my struggles, Ms. ABCD offered to help. I didn't realize that in accepting her help, she was going to do things to imprison me further. I was that ignorant and yes, gullible. I started praying like a warrior. I prayed some more and challenged God to help me. Some people made fun and said I was a fanatic. I didn't let that bother me, I prayed even more. If not for the Lord on my side, I would have been swallowed alive. My early Christian life did not prepare me for this sort of battle. However, I had attended some Charismatic, Pentecostal and Evangelistic churches and services at some stage in my life, mostly by invitation to some special events; and I had seen worshippers gladly worshipping for hours and never once hurrying to leave for some leisurely engagement; and where I saw real deliverances. I had also learnt of God's power of miracles from several Apparitions of the Blessed Virgin Mary. So I believed in the power of God to deliver.

I tried to reach out to a few people around me whom I thought would help; Church leaders, family, and other friends. I soon realized that they didn't understand my predicament, some were suspicious, and others were frankly sure I needed professional help. *"Resist the devil and he will flee from you." James 4:7,* so I told God He must fight for me because I wasn't going to go down.

After several years of suspecting the sources of my trials and tribulations, but didn't have concrete evidence to hold, God showed me in a dream. I confronted this individual, Ms. ABCD, over my dream and finally confirmed the source of the strong demonic attacks over four decades. I confronted her as to my knowledge and drove her out of my life forever, as I relocated to the United States soon after.

WHAT THE HOLY BIBLE SAYS

I believe firmly that God is the same yesterday, today, and forever. He is unchanging, unchangeable and ever living. His awesome power is pronounced for us all "Be still and know that I am God". Every healing of yester-years He repeats today; every battle He fought and won against Satan, He still does today. He exists in the spirit, where we can reach Him only through the spoken words of our prayers. All we need do is call on Him.

According to the Holy Bible, Christ taught and healed the sick. He delivered the oppressed. He fought demonic afflictions; he fed the hungry, and consoled the grieving. He freed the oppressed and saved souls for the kingdom of God, and then handed the same powers over to His church to do these things in His name. These are generally the strategic focus of churches all over the world. There is however some exceptions to the above list of strategic focus; one is *actively fighting demonic and satanic forces, which are working within the communities and churches.* The other is *miracles.* Through miracles which Jesus performed, and through the words of the Holy Bible, he defeated Satan and demonic possessions or oppressions. The Catholic Church and indeed other less known recordings from many Churches, are alive with proven real-life saving miracles, divine encounters, and miraculous healings. Still some churches shy away from calling on the same power of God to fight off satanic attacks against their congregation. In fact there is a near total avoidance of the subject, perhaps to be politically correct, in today's religious discuss. Ordinary laity members do not have information on what steps to take in an encounter with evil forces. There are some which even act as if demons are only in imaginative literature. Please know that demons, wizards and witches are real and dangerous.

A LUKEWARM RESPONSE

The awesome power of God remains consistently manifest in the Catholic Church, the mother church, where authenticated miracles occur regularly and on a global scale. Unfortunately the Church which should lead the Holy war against Satan and his agents has been deliberately incapacitated. First it had been heavily infiltrated worldwide by satanic agents among its congregation, some of who now hold key positions among the laity. In the same way the youth and young adults' population of Christian churches have been alarmingly devastated and somewhat lost to secular and satanic adventurism, while the churches deploy administrative, social and marketing strategies to encourage their greater participation in the churches. In the United States and elsewhere, the widespread sexual scandals reported or unreported, were meant to embarrass, humiliate, incapacitate, and to cause the churches to lose respect and leadership, in order to weaken her for the fight against Satan. The voice of a humiliated leader does not inspire the followership effectively. Other early or later churches have also continued to face crises of financial misappropriation, power tussle, and other kinds of sexual scandals, fractionalization and infiltration. It is for these satanic reasons that the much desired Church unification had remained so far unattainable, no matter how hard members had tried. A house divided cannot stand, let alone firmly engage Satan and his agents in warfare. Surely other Christians have seen this scenario as I have painted here.

Whenever churches had become incapacitated, the respective countries have faced socio-political challenges as a consequence. In such a chaos, satanic forces had been able to operate unhindered and with little resistance from anyone, expanding their influence easily and spreading mayhem as they will. At the same time the Catholic Church, the repository of the divine power discussed above, remains uncomfortably docile or indifferent about tapping and using that divine power to deliver the people of God. Our churches should spend a lot more time, energy and resources including money, on deliverance of the people, for overcoming satanic powers, healing spiritual and physical bondage and teaching strategies against Satan. That is how to touch the deeper problems of the people of God and the society, offering much spiritual freedom. There cannot be meaningful peace and progress in churches and in societies all around the world, until the churches face squarely the satanic attacks against the church of God. The current apparent apathy is not an acceptable option.

All churches should teach their parishioners a lot more about this subject matter and give them what I call 'First Aid' guidance, specifically against demonic attacks; this is preferred to the present state where solutions are shrouded in near total secrecy, if at all. The subject is hardly ever treated in schools or in churches. Frankly, right now, there seems to be a conspiracy of silence, or at best, a lukewarm reaction to this subject. This needs to change. Do the people of God not see how in this situation, Satan and his agents have grown stronger, recruiting the innocents into their societies from right inside churches. Recounting my several problems one day, Ms. ABCD told me rather confidently but gently, that the Catholic Church which I attended was totally powerless and could not help me in my predicament. She then invited me to join her 'white garment church.' Among the West African communities worldwide, as explained by Preachers, and subsequently become well known as an invitation to join a witchcraft society. We had been warned at Church services, against such invitations, and so I declined these invitations four times. On the last occasion, I actually did so very vehemently, and also rather livid at the audacity of her persistence; now realizing I had been put through these trials just for this nefarious objective. Unfortunately for this person, God had previously claimed me for His own purpose. Or was this a test even for me; so that God would know that I truly belonged to Him?

So the typical satanic strategy is to create several crises, problems, difficulties, and challenges in the lives of people, and then, to offer them a solution through this evil society. I am sure that many people in crises might have joined these groups because their churches did not offer any particular solution, support or guidance. Many first, second, third, and subsequent generation churches pretend that demonic forces do not exist and so ignore their debilitating activities in their churches and on their members, who are neither aware nor prepared for the consequences. This is the reason behind the obvious arrogance of the powerful demonic agents who are often tempted to use their powers among innocent, gentle others. Since most of our churches, wanting to be politically correct, have avoided the desired challenge and holy battle which must be fought as Christ did, the Almighty Father started to bring up other Christian churches to take on this critical assignment. I refer here to those truly Christ-focused churches, and not any fake church. The rise of Pentecostal Churches, the subsequent generation churches, and the Praying-warrior-churches, which have remained truly faithful to Christ in doctrine, theology, processes, and practices; was partly a direct consequence of the lethargy of the older generation churches in spiritual warfare. Many observers believe and so do I that God needed new people and churches which would carry on His holy war against Satan. Therefore every true church of Christ should be a payer-warrior church.

Satan truly exists and works through powerful demonic agents. I have watched television programs detailing the antics of such demonic agents all over the world, and their human followers in our midst. These characters are very common in developing countries and referred to as Witches, Wizards, Familiar Spirits, Voodoo agents, Juju priests, Sorcerers, some shades of the Santeria groups etc. Dr. D.K Olukoya (PhD), the Prophet of God, Founder and General Overseer of the Mountain of Fire and Miracles Ministries (MFM) International, has written many prayer books about this topic and had proposed prayer solutions. I have read some of his books and had used the prayers during the holy war of God against my enemies. It is true to state that fighting demonic forces is very dangerous and life threatening. I have seen some unprepared church leaders, Priests, and Pastors, who died suddenly and mysteriously, when they identified or tried to fight off demonic agents and persons in their churches' membership. We must go to God in the spirit and ask Him to take over the battle. We are not equipped to take on the battle on our own. Ours is to pray to God for help. "When God is for us, who can be against us?"

"Who Shall I Send?"

Throughout history, every time political correctness had interfered with the divine mission of churches as directed by God, He had risen up controversy within the church and birthed a more correcting version and generation of the church. The fact that these crises-rebirth-evolutionary cycle had continued through the generations, point to the persistence of evil forces working against the church of God on earth. It also warned of the tendency of churches to focus on the administrative, structural, funding raising, and business management of their churches, with unknown attention to the spiritual battle aspects. I understand that the Catholic Church does have a methodology for response, but this is so submerged under hierarchical machinery, that diagnoses and responses are often slow, hesitant and not widely known. I am not sure how much structure other early generation churches have in this regard. Jesus Christ warned us about demonic attacks, and advised our preparedness. Even He had to face demonic challenges while in the wilderness and at other times during His lifetime. Amazingly, the silence of, and avoidance by most other churches on this topic is deafening and unlike Christ. I also knew and learned from the teachings of my godmother, the late Mrs. Claudiana Obafunke Laotan-Fayemi, a devout practicing Christian, worshipper and servant of God. She often told the story of how the Cherubim and Seraphim Movement Church in Nigeria, was formed out of a divine vision of an angel. A young girl saw the vision of Jesus on the Chalice during the procession of the Corpus Christi celebrations, of the Holy Cross Catholic Church Cathedral, in Lagos, early in the twentieth century. She was reported to have gone into a long term trance, received and relayed historic, divine, extensive, and detailed messages from the Lord leading to the founding of the church. This church today is one of those known for prayer warfare against the devil. There are many more of such recent day churches all over the world. I have heard of some in South America, others in South East Asia, in North America, in Europe, and in Asia. So who will stand up for God and fight the good fight? Who will answer God's call to battle? *John 14: 27b said "Let not your heart be troubled, neither let it be afraid."*

MANIFESTATION OF SATANIC ACTIVITIES

As a consequence of such lethargy against combating demonic agents, these forces have become emboldened, and are easily dissipating the house of God, the Church of Christ on earth. These are some of the manifestation of the attacks on the people of God on earth.

- The final visionary message from the Blessed Virgin Mary at Lourdes warned the world of the likely danger or even death of churches through satanic maneuvers.
- The several sexual scandals and embarrassments of churches.
- The several financial scandals within some churches.
- The several political struggles and scandals within churches.
- The attacks on church leadership and membership.
- The disintegration of some churches and the loss of the younger generations.
- The traumatic encounters by the membership, most of who suffer in silence, not knowing where to turn.
- The avoidance policy of churches which denies the presence of satanic agents on earth.
- The rise of demonic influences in popular culture, media, institutions, and organizations.
- The destructive tendencies in children and the emergence of juvenile killers.
- The rise in the anti-God, anti-Christ voices in our political environments.
- The gradual destruction of moral leadership and authority.
- The susceptibility of the youth, (tomorrow's leaders) to demonic influences.
- The gradual destruction of morality and the rise in openly defiant decadent behavior.
- The upsurge in sociological and psychological crises and disorders.
- The spread of terror and the absence of peace worldwide.

FUTURE—FOCUSED CHURCHES

Many churches are struggling to remain relevant to their congregations. The definition of relevance is also to be carefully defined. Relevance here refers to how the church is able to touch the lives of their members, focus on real spiritual needs for healing, address core emotional and spiritual challenges which the people face, and the churches' abilities to retain membership for a long time.

We should talk about satanic problems, what they are, how they affect people and how people can overcome these, either on their own or within the structures in the churches, at regular gatherings and services. We need to prepare our members to recognize and to withstand any attack of satanic agents such as witches. We should discuss the awesome divine power to overcome and save, and encouraging the use of local experiences. We should open the subject and bring it out of the closet. God gives spiritual powers for a purpose; let us use these to deliver other children of God from ignorance and bondage.

Those churches which focus on the real issues of the people continue to gain membership, while the churches that are being careful about demonic topics, real life challenges of the people, will continue to lose membership, worldwide. What this implies is that our Christian churches will need to gradually relinquish Administration to office support, as the leadership focuses on spiritual healing and deliverance services which combat the devil and his agents, among other spiritual ceremonies for worship, counseling, teaching, sacramental, and thanksgiving etc., in the churches, spiritual healing, teaching, and related activities should be constant and regular features of the churches' existence. Churches must not ignore this major need of the congregation.

It is also a good idea for Christian churches and organizations in different nations to get together, perhaps in a regional or national conference soonest, and devise real strategies against satanic influences and activities in the Christian nations of the world.

GOD IS IN CONTROL

The true Church of Jesus Christ is not a *profit* focused venture. It is a church which brings people to God, prepares them for salvation through grace, heals, delivers, saves, feeds, protects guides, evangelizes, inspires, and carries out all other developmental activities of the church without making any personal profit. To perform God's work at a profit is against the instructions of God. Therefore the religious life of a Priest, Pastor, Teacher, Elder, Bishop, and Prophet and all other such titles, is a divine calling to serve God. It is not a profession to profit from, as in other professional work. Along with this calling comes God's covenant of support. Conversely, anyone not truly called to serve God, cannot do this work successfully. "I am with you", has been a regular assurance, re-assurance, and covenant from God at every turn of my extra-ordinary experiences of the mighty Hand of God over me. Those church leaders who are truly called are given the divine power to combat demonic and satanic forces, and to deliver. We also have the promise of God, that if we knock on His door He will open the door to us; if we seek, we will find; and if we ask, He will give us divine power against demonic forces.

On Sunday May 30, 2010, I had received a spiritual message; "Tell all my churches to start a special prayer session once a week, for all unmarried people who want to be married, so that God may give them victory, remove the hand of the enemy from over them and give them husbands or wives." Through this challenge, satanic sorcerers entice God's children into demonic cults and societies. "The earth is the Lord's and it's fullness thereof," is a promise which tells us that everything belongs to God; it is very easy for him to give to us, all the desires of our hearts while we are on earth, all we need do, is ask God for these blessings. We are not to seek any good from witchcraft or demonic agents. Although they have some powers, they cannot save, they destroy and deceive; and lead their followers straight to hell and damnation. God's amazing power has brought me so far. I am confident that He will continue to sustain me. The Lord God Almighty has not finished with me. He has a lot more work for me to do to tell of His powers over all creation and to honor His Holy name.

CHAPTER 11

The Person's Roles In Spiritual Warfare

Introduction

Each person must develop respective spiritual prowess and get a direct line to God. We came into the world on our own, as individuals. The prayers of others, of parents, or friends, and of support groups can help immensely. However, a time will come when the person himself must get involved in reaching out to God. This is a situation that we cannot fight by ourselves. I wish our churches would preach and talk about existential dangers of evil demonic or satanic agents. It is by doing so that they would guide us and prepare the community for any such attacks in the future. Not to do so, is to keep us helpless and unprepared for the dangers ahead, since no one knows when one may meet such dangers; it is expedient to be prepared and ready. In our daily or regular prayer sessions at homes, in churches, and in prayer groups, we must also be aware, sensitive and prayerfully ready.

My experiences

I openly confess that in the first quarter of my life, I was most unprepared for the encounter. Now I looked back, God had put me in two situations where I should have become more spiritually attuned to Him. Unfortunately, I didn't take up the invitations seriously. My roommate at the university was a born-again Christian, who tried, but found it impossible to introduce me to her lifestyle. At the National

Youth Service in 1976, I met and was drawn to a Christian couple, through whom I actually saw the power of God at work in ordinary humans like us. I had gone to a prayer meeting with them at a Flying school in the outskirts of the town, when, at the end of the meeting, they prayed for transportation back to our camp. Just as we started the long walk back towards the highway, a friend showed up in a car and asked to give us a ride. I was astounded and saw God's intervention in our daily lives from that day. I saw the result of answered prayers. This experience stayed with me up till today. My third experience was the case reported when I attended the Businessmen's Gospel breakfast event. Nothing in my previous religious life prepared me or told me that witchcraft dangers were real. In fact whereas the society talked about it, my church and schools never discussed it, and further encouraged us to think and behave as if they don't exist. In other words, such talks were either idle gossip or talks by heathens. I now know that these teachings were dead wrong. I hope that families would read my book and learn early about the dangers around, and run to God early. *Apparently, I needed to draw nearer to God, so that I could be prepared for the journey in which the Lord was to take me.*

WHAT THE HOLY BIBLE SAYS

The first thing to do is to pray for the Spirit of Discernment. Pray also for God to sharpen your spiritual and bodily sense, so that you would see what you need to see, hear what you need to hear, and know what you need to know. Then ask God to take over the battle for you. The enemy will dull your senses, cover your eyes, and try to prevent you realizing what is going on in your life. Remember these are destructive principalities you are up against. *1 Peter 5:7 "Casting all your care upon Him, for He cares for you"*, and in Psalm 50:15, God invites us to come to Him at such times. *"Call upon me in the day of trouble; I will deliver you, and you shall glorify me." "In my distress, I cried to the Lord, and He heard me. Deliver my soul, O Lord, from lying lips and from deceitful tongue." Psalm 120: 1-2.* The whole of Psalm 124:1-8, describes the salvation of God for the man who called on God, when he was besieged by evil doers. Hannah also prayed and said, *"My heart exults in the Lord; my strength is exulted in the Lord. My mouth derides my enemies, because I rejoice in thy salvation." 1 Samuel 2: 1.* The only grace for victory is in the Lord our God. Run to Him when in trouble with wicked men and women. Pray like a warrior, in the morning, afternoon evening and night. All the time, pray without ceasing for His deliverance. He will answer you.

SATANIC & DEMONIC ATTACKS

Satanic attacks are deliberate, sustained and debilitating, wearing the target out and down. They are **real** and are weapons of spiritual warfare, frequently deployed by witches or sorcerers to annihilate their opponents. The attacks often lead to sudden death, aligned with some normal causes. They may focus on body organs, body parts or the entire body. They are stressful, causing anxiety, pain, depression, panic attacks, and lack of peace; unexplained fear and sorrow; and destroying self-confidence. It usually takes a long time before the target is able to understand, then explain or discuss with others what is going on. One may not even know who is responsible. So the person internalizes the problem. The more one internalizes the problem, the more compounded the crisis becomes; and the more destructive to the spirit, soul and body. They operate in the unseen spirit realm where humans do not operate normally, except through prayers and the spoken word, taking advantage of ones sensory inefficiencies.

Why they attack. They attack to exercise and gain more power, to gain control of human destinies, for personal benefit and gains, to carry out demonic instructions, to take over lives, to eliminate the lives of their adversaries at will, and to gain unfair and undue advantage over others. They virtually gain the power to determine who lives and who dies.

How do they attack? How do we know that one is under satanic attacks? The following list is not exhaustive for sure, but only points to some examples. Satanic agents attack through bizarre or frightening nightmares, regular dreams, dreams of lizards, cats, dogs, lions, or other wild animals. When the target attends social or wedding ceremonies in dreams, has sexual intercourse in dreams, when snake-like, or worm-like forms enter the body in dream or half wakefulness, when the person eats food in dreams, when the person is being chased in dreams. When one is in a gathering, in church or on a queue, watch out for all those who sit behind you, sending curses through silent voices. A lady had invited me to attend a Thanksgiving service for a recovering third party. In good conscience, I attended, not realizing the two women were cult associates of Ms. ABCD in the United States. During the several mini thanksgivings, I had gone up to give my contributions. By the time of the concluding general thanksgiving, I didn't have any more money to give, and so decided not to go for this final one. Earlier as we had arrived, this lady had sat us down such that when it was time for thanksgiving, she would be standing behind me. She was so taken aback when I declined to go for the final thanksgiving procession, that for a while she kept on insisting I got up with her. Finally I confronted her as she stood there in church, to ask if there was more to this than meets the eye, at which point she gave up. I saw and heard her whisper quietly behind me on our way out of the church later that day. I only smiled because I had previously soaked and covered myself with the blood of Jesus, so that all curses were returned to the sender. Please watch out and be constantly on the alert. They curse you discretely when your back is turned, in churches, pews, homes and at socials. Avoid people touching your head for any reason or helping you tie scarves, head gear during ceremonies, or to put your cap on your head. Sexual intercourse in dreams is a definite sign of demonic attack and violation, no matter whose face you see or whose body is lying down with you. It is not a romantic, helpless wishful desire for sex. No it is a terrible demonic attack. Pray to God immediately, and seek help later if you can.

We may not know the details of how they do what they do, but we have seen and know some of their activities on others; to ignore or deny these would be disadvantageously myopic

- They can interfere with marital relationships and unions, in any way they please.
- They can destroy pregnancies and prevent childbearing.
- They can frustrate business success, or scheme to offer temporary business success.
- They can destroy professional success.
- They can cause physical and mental ill health, e.g. blindness.
- They can kill the body, but not the soul.
- They can cause financial failure; be careful about joint business ventures.

- They can cause major misfortunes.
- They can cause educational failures.
- They can control the spirit of a person, keeping their soul in bondage and their body subservient, controlling the thoughts, actions and life of the person.

They are able to do these destructive things and more, only if the target is not in the strong hands of God. In their demonic nature, they don't know who is their parent, brother, sister, cousin, child, relation or friend. Loyalty to the cult is paramount, they pursue their goal relentlessly, and everyone else is fair game. At first I didn't know what I was seeing, but now understand better. I have seen brothers of witches suffer professionally, one business after another crashing needlessly, sisters suffered childless pains, siblings in marital problems until coerced into the cult, many family friends who died suddenly, one after the other, another becoming very sick and nearly died, people and family members, backing away violently from the known witch, ignorant suitors trapped into marriages with satanic girls. I have seen sexual predator-teachers and lecturers who died suddenly. I saw sexually adventurous men died suddenly. I have seen demonic turf wars in business organizations; and respective wives dying suddenly, or children suffering as a result. I have seen happy homes destroyed suddenly and/or taken over by an evil agent. They use and discard innocent poor souls as battering rams. I have seen so called difficult husbands who died suddenly, others become totally subdued suddenly. I have seen where a woman would visit a friend at home put something in the home and create violent tension between the couple, until they separated and divorced so as to isolate and attract the wife into witchcraft. I have seen with the spiritual eye, a field full of about one thousand young children recently introduced into witchcraft, but later delivered by the blood of Jesus. Witches attack one's blessings, they divert goodness, they create tension, strife and anxiety, they break up relationships, they introduce harm, they have evil powers to enter into peoples' bodies and damage the physiology, they create barrenness, they cause blindness, and they kill remotely. They can and often imprison a person's spirit, and make that person their perpetual slave, and controlling the fortunes of the person. I am sure they do a lot more damage than listed here. They do these in secret, and quietly; and the most uncanny thing is they do so remotely. That is why they are very successful, and unreachable by the law or the person. These demonic agents put various obstacles before the person to stop, postpone or steal the blessings intended for the person. They attack the person in dreams, which make the person feeling tense upon waking up. Dr. D.K Olukoya(PhD), the Prophet of God, Founder and General Overseer of the Mountain of Fire and Miracles Ministries MFM International, has also written many books over satanic dreams and how satanic agents have manipulated the lives of people into disaster and failure through dream attacks. In these ways they introduce demonic objects into the body of the person.

At a period in my life, I suddenly started to feel that there was something moving inside my body, on the left lower abdomen. From time to time, I felt this form in body movements, as if a living creature, like a huge snake was moving around in that part of my body. I was scared and worried and didn't know where to turn. I didn't know how to explain to my doctor that I have a moving object in my body, which I sometimes feel whenever I was laying down; and sometimes did not feel it. One day, as I prayed for divine healing over this moving object, the Holy Spirit instructed me to put my hand over the area where this creature was in my body as it was moving around, and pray over it. As I did so, warmth came over my hands, then onto the spot on my left abdomen. Immediately, the moving object stopped, and I have never felt the movements of the object again. I couldn't and didn't discuss this with anyone. I didn't know who to tell and how to tell anyone. So I kept quiet, until now. I realized something evil was introduced into my body purposely to cause damage. But the power of God destroyed the evil, removed the object and delivered me. A word for parents; as our pastors have advised often, pray always with your children, teach them to get closer to God, in all ways possible. Know and be assured that God exists. Know that evil exists too, and looking for new disciples and the unprotected children are extremely vulnerable. Pray and watch who their friends are, which homes they visit. Cover them constantly with the blood of Jesus, so that this goes with them everywhere they go. Trust no one with your children. We are traditionally careful with strangers, but hardly ever with known people. Be careful you do not bring artifacts, paintings, sculptures or symbols of demonic or satanic images, and links into your home. Watch out for jewelry in shapes of snakes, in any form.

From a young age, guide them away from inappropriate films, books, video, and other games, activities of satanic rituals, witchcraft, and demonic characters to which they are exposed everywhere, and in schools where they meet children from generational witchcraft families. Get involved in their lives and some of their activities. Know your children closely.

The rest of the world should stop glamourizing evil, the demonic, and the satanic. Parents should do something constructive, advocate for positive healthy 'Change' in our streets, areas, counties, local government areas, and circles of influence. Parents are still the first and best teachers for their children. You owe them a good example to follow. "Teach your children the good path to follow when they are young and they will not depart from it when they are older." Parents should teach their children about demonic forces at play, and teach the children some elements of prayer warfare however basic, gradually expanding such skills as the children grow older. I have also seen the sudden vengeance of God on these evil agents. I have seen them face God's wrath and judgment, one after another. I have seen them inside the pit they had dug for the innocent, and the evil which they planned, became their own portion. Although they are strong with evil power, God is mightier and stronger. I have seen them in total fear, once they realized that they face a divine power greater than anything they have. To God be the glory forever and ever.

GET A DIRECT LINE TO GOD.

This is a direct communication line to God, so much so that one will hear the voice of God as He talks to the person. When one raises her voice to Him, He recognizes the person's voice, name, and face. Build a relationship with God. Pray to Him, sing to Him, talk to Him, praise Him, worship Him, adore Him, love Him and get His arms around you. *Psalm 5: 3 "My voice You shall hear in the morning O Lord; In the morning I will direct it to You, and I will look up."* It is only when we are in the hands of God that the enemy cannot touch, or harm us. When we seek God early in the morning, He appreciates it, values the effort to wake up and call on Him at dawn. Several times in the Holy Bible, He promises exceptional attention to those who rise up early in the morning, just for His sake. *Psalm 119:147 "I rise before the dawning of the morning, and cry for help. I hope in Your word"*. Once one is in the habit of calling God, of praying to Him and hearing His response, the person can no longer stop. The person will want to reach Him all the time, and then throughout your life. I am amazed at King David, who remains an example to emulate. He turned and spoke to God at every turn; when faced with big issues and with small issues. He had a familiarity with God that one would always admire, and God loved Him, faults and all. His was not just a direct line but a hot line to God.

The hotline comes through prayers! Prayers! Prayers! Prayers! Prayers! Prayers and Prayers! In all the many books written by all authors against this subject or on account of any spiritual matter, prayers take the center-stage. Prayer is the hotline to God. Prayer is how to seek, and obtain deliverance, and freedom from satanic forces. Prayers get you God's ears; and then things begin to happen for you through the mercy and grace of God.

Experienced writers, sages and folktales, tell us that those who are near are often the most dangerous. Someone said once that a person, who doesn't know you, has nothing to get, gain or take from you. He doesn't know what one does, what one has or does not have, and what one's plans are. Something else, one cannot be as careful as the stalker is as cunning. One can only do so much. That is why these close enemies do a major damage to the target. However, no matter how clever they are, the wisdom of God is greater. That is why every machination of enemies, God turns round and onto themselves. They usually think they are cleverer in their schemes, but before God, they are dumb. Please be alert when God is warning you about dangers from close associates. Contrary to popular belief, demonic agents may be among acquaintances, casual contacts, neighbors, business associates, work colleagues, schools mates and even families. Be prayerful and watchful. Listen more, see more, think more, feel more and most of all pray more. In my case I met one at a school sports day. Later on I understood that a certain family had sent this girl to target me for their own purpose. Later, she took over the 'case' for her own advantage when she realized I was an easy prey at the beginning. They made the greatest mistake of their lives because God had anointed me as His own, even before I came to earth.

So, it turned out that I was taken through about forty-two years of harrowing experiences, so as to break me, and when that didn't work, so as to weaken me for what was coming—the demonic invitation to join a 'white garment church'; which term we understand and were warned as an invitation into witchcraft cult. I recall all the things denied me, all the sufferings I went through, all the pain I suffered, all the humiliation I endured, all the tears, blood, and sweat. I suffered numerous denials in life and faced multiple obstacles; just so that I would have been so distraught, and broken that I would be an easy prey or would jump at the invitation to membership. Ms. ABCD didn't realize that God already owned me, and was not about to release me to the devil or his agents. Over the years, she had quietly dropped this invitation to me, but which I had declined, first thinking she was talking about some of the white garment churches we have around. By the fourth and last time she made the invitation, I knew what she was inviting me into and I was ready for her. I questioned her why she had not relented in making these invitations after I had declined several times earlier. I told her firmly never to make this invitation to me again. I told her I am a child of God covered in the blood of Jesus. I then stopped all interactions with her. Many men and women who had wanted something very badly in their lives, and who were unsuspecting of satanic wars holding back their blessings, would have been similarly invited to join the cult in order to gain the benefit. I wonder how many other children of God might have been tricked, enticed, or harassed into sorcery, witchcraft or demonic alliances, by similar means. Their membership is growing astronomically. On Thursday July 31, 2008, the voice of God said to me "Tell the single people of the world who want spouses, to ask me for what they want husband or wife and I will give them, but they must depart from sin of adultery and fornication". I am conveying that message here.

Everyone should be concerned about these situations. Is there any wonder that unrighteous behavior is not only encouraged all over the world, but excused and covered up, even advocated in some quarters? This is so much so that the guilty party is excused and the innocent is condemned. Unrighteousness is unholy as we all know, so who will stand up for God? I refer to recent media stories about demonic cults of youngsters and other older members. These call for quick intervention by parents, churches, schools and the society who must prepare our children, members and students by teaching them some basic responses to demonic attacks and influences. Although there are open and growing influences of sorcery in societies, the responses of concerned adults, responsible adults, and others, appear inadequate.

PRAYER FOUND UNDER CHRIST'S SEPULCHRE (1583 AD).

"O God Almighty, who suffered death upon the cross particularly for my sins, be with me. Holy Cross of Jesus have pity on me. Holy Cross of Jesus be my protector. Holy Cross of Jesus, take away all bitter pains. Holy Cross of Jesus, take away all evil. Holy Cross of Jesus let me walk in the way of salvation. Preserve me from all temporal accidents; take away any danger of certain death. I always adore the Holy Cross of Jesus Christ. Jesus of Nazareth crucified, have pity on me. Make the spirit of evil leave me for all times.

Oh Mother of Perpetual Succour, I come before Thy Sacred Picture, and with a child-like conscience invoke Thine aid. Show Thyself a Mother to me now; Have pity on me. Oh dearest Mother of Perpetual Succour, for the love Thou bearest to Jesus and in honour of His sacred wounds, help me in this my necessity; (Mention it). Oh Loving Mother, I leave it all to Thee in the Name of the Father, I leave it all to Thee in the Name of the Son, I leave it all to Thee in the Name of the Holy Spirit. Amen. OUR LADY OF PERPETUAL SUCCOUR, PRAY FOR US. (3times)"

(This prayer was sent by the Pope to Charles when he went to fight the enemy of France. J.C.O.E.M 17.6.1992)

---≼ CHAPTER 12 ≽---

DIVINE DELIVERANCE

INTRODUCTION

"Who is greater than Jehovah-El-Shaddai? There is no one greater than Jehovah-El-Shaddai". This is the title of a popular song in one of the churches I attended while in Nigeria. It is a declaration that there is no power greater than Jehovah's. Incidentally this was my parting quotation to Ms. ABCD sometime in 2008, and before I returned to the United States. At that moment I was no longer afraid of her powers because I knew that however powerful she was, (and she was devastatingly powerful from experiences which I had seen of others around her and of mine), the power of God is immeasurably bigger and stronger. I knew my deliverance had been completed by then, and all I had to do was obey God's directives to the letter. I knew that it was God Almighty fighting my battles. Unfortunately, I was unable to convince those around me that the power they saw was not mine, but the power of God. I tried to tell some people but stopped after a while as they were not easily convinced. I declare to the world that God is alive, strong, and powerful. I am back to my original statement; God is the same yesterday, today and tomorrow. The God of Daniel in the den of lions is alive. The God of Moses before the power of Pharaoh is alive. The God of David before the Goliath is alive. How I wish those who tried His power would come out and confess to what they did and to what God did to them. Of course they would normally not do so unless God wants to ridicule them before the world. He would strike them suddenly from behind and they would become disgraced, dishonored forever and ever. You will recall that in Luke 10:19, the Lord God of Moses said *"Behold, I give you the authority*

112

to trample on all serpents and scorpions, and over all the power of the enemy, and nothing shall by any means hurt you." The powerful words of God are sacrosanct and are life.

WHAT THE HOLY BIBLE SAYS

The Apostle Paul assures us in *Ephesians 6:10-13 that "Finally, my brethren, be strong in the Lord and in the power of His might. Put on the armor of God that you may be able to stand against the wiles of the devil; for we do not wrestle against flesh and blood, but against the rulers of the darkness of this age, against spiritual hosts of wickedness in the heavenly places. Therefore take up the whole armor of God that you may be able to withstand in the evil day, and having done all, to stand."* By the grace of God, we will stand tall.

It was sometime on March 15, 2008, that the word of God came to me; *"I am the God of Daniel, the God of Moses and the God of David".* He told me He was the one taking over the battle. Mark you, He didn't send an angel; He didn't send another divine entity. God Himself took over this battle. My enemies were doomed for generations and generations. To be faced with the immense power of God is certain decimation, total disintegration. Conversely, the powers which held the child of God in severe bondage for about forty-two years must have been terrible, so much so that God Himself rose up in anger against my enemies. He asked me to sit and watch what He would do to all of them. From this time on He spoke to me directly, I didn't need an interpreter. He showed me what I needed to see. I became a different person. The Spirit of God surrounded me totally. I became a new person in God the Father, Son and Holy Spirit. I saw others who had been silent adversaries revealed in their true forms—just as He promised to show me. He then gave me His mission for my destiny. I am on that road now and will never depart from it. It is a mission which I am very happy to accept. Those who still wish to test God's power are free to do so to their own peril. *"I am who I am." Exodus 3:4* was His reply to Moses when he asked who God was, so he could tell the Israelites in Egypt. This is a name like no other name. *Psalm 72:17 says "His name shall endure forever; His name shall continue as long as the sun. And men shall be blessed by Him; all nations shall call Him blessed."*

It is a pity that some people do not really know God, in His majesty and might; they do not believe in Him, they do not understand His power, omnipotence or immensity. Such people are living lives of pretense; and fooling no one but themselves; they become easy prey to demonic agents around. If we truly know God, we would not do harm, we would serve and worship only the Almighty God; we would obey all His laws to the letter, show respect, and avoid doing evil.

AWARENESS OF DANGER

It is impossible to be as cunning as the one who is plotting danger, while wearing the cloak of friendship. It is impossible to be aware of danger from the one who lives with you, eats with you, and shares your secret pains and struggles, while plotting death. It is initially impossible to identify the 'frenemy', a contemporary term which means an enemy who presents himself or herself as a friend; who plots death for you, or who steals valuable blessings from you, under the cloak of sharing.

One Sunday early in 2007, as I was about to leave for Mass, Ms. ABCD had stopped by my house without notice, saying she was on her way to church and wanted to show me a new car; she had parked it outside and asked me to come out to see the car. Immediately the Holy Spirit warned me that something was not right about this unexpected visit and my senses became heightened, adrenalin flowed through my veins at the same time, as if there was danger. I said a short prayer of protection and followed her outside. As I stepped outside my gate with her, I looked up and saw four young boys, not more than eighteen years old, in rough looking suits, standing across from my gate on the other side of the street; they didn't fit into the environment, in spite of their obvious borrowed attire meant to conceal their true nature, and I realized they were hired Assassins. I remained unruffled, calmly went to see the car and then walked right across the street to meet the boys. I asked them, their mission as they loitered, and their names, their addresses in the Estate where I lived, and warned them I was reporting them all to the security gate. One of them said they came from a certain house in the area, and I asked for the name of their parents, since I was a member of the Estate Association for some time and knew all families on my street. He failed to respond at all. The Holy Spirit which directed my steps and actions took control and led me to talk to them. This must have shocked them. I left them and returned into the house but took security precautions immediately, and for the next few weeks, before I travelled out of the country.

Ms. ABCD tried but failed to kill me through witchcraft, she tried but failed to cause mental health problems, and she tried but failed to kill me through Assassins. Every day of life, it is the Lord who protects. The watchman watches in vain, unless the Lord keeps safe. One thing we can do during our respective prayers is to ask God to open our eyes to see the dangers around us. When He heightens our spirit, we become aware of dangers in our environment. Nothing can be hidden or done in secret to us anymore.

Psalm 18: 2 "The Lord is my rock and my fortress and my deliverer; My God my strength in whom I trust; my shield and the horn of my salvation; my stronghold." It was this rock that protected me. It was in this fortress that God took me and shielded me. The strong arm of God became my portion. His righteous right hand smote my enemies down one by one. He is and was the shield of salvation which guarded me on the right and on the left. He was the horn of salvation which stood firm as my stronghold. God has not finished with my enemies. Only if they turn from their wickedness would they survive. *Luke 1: 68, "Blessed is the Lord God of Israel, (my God and Father) for He has visited and redeemed His people (me)." Isaiah 44:22*

For many years I was at war but didn't know it. I was naïve, trusting, and even foolish. Many unexpected, strange, and tense events, activities, and even deaths around me, had great implications for me, but I wasn't aware of the danger to me and my family. I didn't see the danger until God opened my eyes. I needed to see with the eye of the Holy Spirit. I needed the Holy Spirit to give me complete understanding, knowledge, and wisdom so that I would see the whole picture, so that I would understand the relationships that tied these events together; the knowledge to discern what the enemy was doing even though in secret; and so that I would have the wisdom to see how they were affecting me. God also began to teach me by Himself, His wisdoms from the Holy Bible. *"For You, are my rock and my fortress, therefore for Your name's sake, Lead me and guide me." Psalm 31:3. "Now thanks be to God who always leads us in triumph in Christ, and through us diffuses the fragrance of His knowledge in every place." 2 Corinthians 2:14.*

During the period of bondage, I felt constant physical tension, I was depressed, I suffered anxiety about life, I was afraid of the unseen hand controlling my life. I was isolated because there was no one to share my problems with. I could hardly even articulate all my experiences in a coherent manner, for a third party to understand, and offer help. I went through repeated periods of insomnia. I went from one crisis to another. Over and over, I recall wondering out loud to some people around me, and asking who would want to harm me, in my state of struggles. I didn't have much, or the kind of luxurious life that anyone would envy or want, I thought. I was so wrong. Over and over again, I had dreams of danger, in one form or another. I didn't understand what some of the dreams meant initially. I even thought that the dreams were silly and meaningless. Also I would forget some dreams when I woke up, but only remember the feeling of tension upon waking up.

I wondered why my life appeared to be in chaos. Every point of prayer appeared not being answered or frustrated, yet I know that God answers prayers. I was talking too much into the hands of the enemies, about my difficulties because I didn't have anyone else to share my pains with. I didn't realize that many of these persons were the deadly enemies. I was going from problem to problem and was being drowned in them. I was often disoriented and confused. My only reality and consolation was the prayer sessions I had daily and every Tuesday special sessions with my children. These and my professional work became the only activities that made sense.

As a result of these experiences, my first thought was that perhaps I was being punished by God for my many failings. So I prayed harder. I tried to change my behavior; I doubled my efforts at kind words and deeds. I started to seek after more of God's righteousness. At this time, I started to attend early morning Mass as I left for work every day. I also looked for the company of praying Christians, and thinking that I would learn some things to give me better understanding of what I was going through. You will recall that since no one had ever described to me what witchcraft attack or bondage felt or looked like, I didn't know. *Psalm 71: 4 "Deliver me O God out of the hands of the wicked; Out of the hands of the unrighteous and cruel man"*

AGAINST EVIL FORCES

Over the years, I had heard Preachers list factors which are required for some subject they were discussing. In this write up, I want to list these seven for total victory against witchcraft in any form. 1) The Holy arm of God covering you; 2) The blood of Jesus over you; 3) The knowledge of the Holy Spirit guiding you; 4) The prayers of Mother Mary for support; 5) The sword of St Michael the Archangel which is guarding you; 6) The Prayer of Angels for you, and 7) Your holy anger, faith, and cry energizing you. In 2Thessalonica 3:3 *"But the Lord is faithful, who will establish you and guard you, both that you do and will do the things we command you."* The Apostle Paul gave us the divine assurance to strengthen our resolve, and faith in God against evil forces. He tells us further in *Ephesians 6:10 "Finally my brethren, be strong in the Lord and in the power of His might."* Turn to God. He is stronger, mightier, and greater than evil powers.

In doing all these, with the grace of God, you will overcome. *"Let God arise, Let His enemies be scattered; Let those also who hate Him flee before Him." Psalm 68: 1.*

Our greatest sacrifice is thanksgiving before the Lord God. *"Therefore by Him let us continually offer the sacrifice of praise to God, that is, the fruit of our lips, giving thanks to His name." Hebrews 13:15.* Remember the covenants of God remain forever; and also remember that prayer works through total faith, trust, and submission to God. *Isaiah 26:3 "You will keep him in perfect peace, whose mind is stayed on You, because he trusts in You. Trust in the Lord forever, for in YAH, the Lord is everlasting strength."* Seek God diligently and persevere to the end. God said to us *"I love those who love me, and those who seek Me diligently will find Me." Proverbs.8:17.* In my journey, I was led to use this prayer daily, and so recommend the prayer also to you.

Prayer to defeat the work of Satan

"O Divine Eternal Father, in union with your Divine Son and the Holy Spirit, and through the Immaculate Heart of Mary, I beg you to destroy the power of your greatest enemy—(Satan and) the evil Spirits. Cast them into the deepest recess of hell and chain them there forever! Take possession of your kingdom which you have created and which is rightfully yours. Heavenly Father, give us the reign of the Sacred Heart of Jesus and the Immaculate Heart of Mary. I repeat this prayer out of pure love for You with every beat of my heart and with every breath I take. Amen." (March 1973. Richard H. Ackerman, Bishop of Covington.) *This prayer is reproduced with permission of the publishers, the Miraculous Lady of the Roses. Michigan. 49060. USA.*

This is the assurance of God to us when we call on him in trials such as I have described in this book. *Romans 16:20 "And the God of grace will crush Satan under your feet shortly. The grace of our Lord Jesus Christ be with you. Amen."*

Thanksgiving in War and Victory

Let us emulate the Apostle Paul and give God thanks. *". . . But thanks be to God who gives us the victory through our Lord Jesus Christ."* *1Corinthians15:57.* Copy the example of the Psalmist and thank God. *"To the end that my glory may sing praise to you and not be silent. O Lord my God, I will give thanks to You forever."* Broadcast His faithfulness so that the world would know WHO God is; *Psalm 30:12. "I will sing of the mercies of the Lord forever; with my mouth will I make known Your faithfulness to all generations."* Psalm 89:1. This is what I have been doing in recent years. Even this book is in honor and thanksgiving to God for His immense love for me. If I have a thousand tongues, they would not be enough to give you thanks O God.

"How precious is Your loving kindness O God?" Psalm 36:7. "Let them praise His name with the dance; Let them sing praises to Him with the timbrel and harp." Psalm 149:3. "You have turned for me my mourning into dancing: You have put off my sackcloth and clothed me with gladness." Psalm 30:11. "Sing, O heavens, for the Lord has done it! Shout, you lower

parts of the earth; Break forth into singing, you mountains, O forest and every tree in it! For the Lord has redeemed Jacob (me), and glorified Himself in Israel." Isaiah 44:23. "The Lord is my strength and my shield; in him my heart trusts; so I am helped, and my heart exults, and with my song I give thanks to him." Psalm 28:7. Also and finally in *Psalm 150: 1-6,* is a song of thanksgiving and everlasting praise to God. The words of the Holy Bible are living words of God, which go out of the mouth and achieve the intention of the divine statement. Speak Biblical words as often as one needs to and for all purposes in one's life.

....

CONCLUSION

'A life of Divine Victory'-this is the promise of God to us all. This can be your portion too.

"For by grace you have been saved through faith, and that not of yourselves; it is the gift of God." Ephesians 2:8.

Between 1968 and 2010, I went through about forty-two years of bondage, pain, humiliation, trials, tribulations, tears, demonic attacks, witchcraft oppression, physical afflictions, and psychological terrors of day and night. I also experienced warfare of tongues, rumors, slanders, gossip in a persistent and relentless manner. It took me a long time to realize I was facing strong demonic forces of evil, fighting to destroy me. I had no control whatsoever and couldn't stop the deluge of spiritual and demonic warfare. I prayed like a warrior and the crises would subside only to resurface again, stronger than the last episodes. I continued daily prayers, three hourly prayers, fasting and praise-songs, and staying on the saving covenants of God. I visited and prayed to God at the Altar of our Blessed Mother Mary at the Shrine of the Sacred Heart in N.W. Washington D.C and asked her help to carry my plea to God. In an amazing dream the next day, she instructed me what to do. I did as instructed; and the power of God, the Blood of Jesus, and the inspiration of the Holy Ghost, delivered me from all evil. God overcome all the attacks, and I was delivered from all oppression, as God Himself took full control of my life and destiny, and reaffirmed my life as a life of divine victory.

Who knows, perhaps it was for such an assignment that the Lord God Jehovah took me through the harrowing experiences, protected and spared my life. Therefore to the one, holy, immortal, and eternal God, be honor, glory, authority, dominion, and power.

I have His covenant in Isaiah 49:25 & 26 "Even the captives of the mighty shall be taken away, and the prey of the terrible shall be delivered; for I will contend with they that contend with thee and I will save thy children. And I will feed them that oppress you with their own flesh and they shall be drunken with their own blood as with sweet wine; and all flesh shall know that I the Lord I'm thy Savior and thy Redeemer, the Mighty one of Jacob." These bible verses and covenants continue to be fulfilled in my life every day. When God is for us, who can be against us?

BLESSED BE GOD FOREVER

"Daniel answered and said: Blessed be the name of God forever and ever. For wisdom and might are His." Daniel 2:20. This is what to do after God has revealed secrets, brought salvation, and deliverance to us. It is by the grace of God that we have continued to survive trials and tribulations. It is by God's grace that we are where we are today; and it is by His grace that we have victory upon victory. It was He who fought all our battles. Like Daniel, I could never have survived all the tests, all the attacks and eventually the lions' den, but for the powerful right hand of God. When people go through life's crises, we often don't look at spiritual problems as we consider physical sources and therefore possible solutions. It is amazing how many lives have been destroyed by this oversight. I contend that we should consider all possible sources of problems and address them from all angles. I learnt the hard way. I urge us to consider the following:

1. Holding onto God: No one else can solve our spiritual problems but God. The challenge now is how to turn people back to focusing on the spiritual, as against the carnal. Once people do this, half the battle is won. I suggest that our Churches who have been doing a good job would need to continue this effort. To hold on to God, we must continue to pray, praise, worship, thank and be in His presence.

2. Doing His will: Wherever we are at all times, obey him and trust His directives, build up faith knowing that He exists, truly loving and caring for us, and protecting us from danger. Whatever He commands us to do; we do in the struggle for survival.

Sometimes His instructions might look odd to human life, but please do so. When the prophet Elisha instructed Naaman, the Syrian Army Commander and a leper to wash seven times in the river Jordan, he became cured on the seventh wash, even though he didn't see the point of the exercise initially. *2Kings 5:14.* Ours is to obey completely even if it doesn't make any sense to us immediately.

3. Moving closer to God and resisting the devil: Remember that in such battles, one is often alone in the war except for God. No one will come and fight one's spiritual battles, just as for other kinds of battles. Therefore whatever one's lifestyle had been before now, the person needs to transform and move closer to God.

4. Striving for purity: To be able to move closer to God effectively, one must aim to be righteous. Being mere mortals, the best we can do is to try to be pure and blameless, because only God is pure and blameless. Only He is good, and only He is pure. *Matthew 5:8 "Blessed are the pure in heart, for they shall see God." Some text says "Blessed are the pure in spirit, for they shall see God."*

5. Pursuing righteousness: This is the path that leads to purity. To me, this means doing what is right in the eyes of God, at every turn. It may be difficult to do; it may be unpleasant, people might talk and gossip, they might castigate you, criticize you for it, but your focus must be only on God.

6. Proclaiming His wonders: When you have seen the mighty powers of God, His awesome hand of deliverance, you will want to talk about it. You will want to tell the whole world. Whatever your reasons are, you will broadcast it. It is joy to be a special child of God, whose salvation and deliverance is your portion.

7. Encouraging others: We are our brothers' (and sisters') keepers. Many people are living in limbo not knowing what is going on around them or in their lives. Each of us was created to support

and help our neighbor in any way we can, when he/she needs our help. Perhaps the reason for one's encounter with that person was so that we could touch them positively. So offer your hand of support to others, and encourage them to seek divine help in crises.

8. Giving thanks to God: My name *Modupe, pronounced Mo-du-pe,* is a Yoruba word which is translated as 'I give thanks' or 'Thanksgiving'. I really do thank God for the victories he gave me, in all the above narration and much more.

A Prayer of Thanksgiving

So you see, God is the same unchanging Authority, yesterday, today and tomorrow; now you too can call on Him. Let us pray:

In the name of Jesus! In the name of Jesus! In the name of Jesus! Bless the Lord O my soul. O lord my God you are very great. You are clothed with honor and majesty. Before the mountains were brought forth, or ever you had formed the earth and the world, from everlasting to everlasting you are God. For in you all things were created in heaven and on earth, visible and invisible, whether thrones or dominions or principalities or authorities—all things were created through you and for you. You are before all things and in you all things hold together. Holy! Holy! Holy! Is the Lord of hosts, the whole earth is full of your glory. Your steadfast love Lord, never ceases, your mercies never come to an end; they are new every morning. Your covenants are my shield. Your promises remain constant. I was a captive of the mighty but you took me away from them. I was a prey of the terrible but you delivered me. You then contended with all those who contended with me; you saved my children. All those who oppressed me, you fed with their own flesh, and they became drunk with their own blood as with sweet wine, and all flesh knew that you, the Lord Jehovah, are my Savior and my Redeemer-the Mighty one of Jacob. Omnipotent God of Daniel, you fought the lions for me; God of Moses, you destroyed the powers of the demons, witches and satanic agents of pharaoh, who attacked and oppressed me; God of David, you vanquished the Goliaths who vowed to destroy me; for you are my refuge, a strong tower against the enemy. Who is greater than Jehovah El-Shaddai? No one is greater than

Jehovah El-Shaddai. Let the heavens be glad, and let the earth rejoice, and let them say among the nations 'the Lord reigns'. Be exalted O God above the heavens, and your glory above all the earth. Truly! Lord God of hosts, you are my shepherd, therefore I shall not want. You make me lie down in green pastures. You lead me beside still waters, you restore my soul. You lead me in paths of righteousness for your name's sake. Even though I walk through the valley of the shadow of death, I fear no evil because you are always with me. Your rod and your staff are my comfort. Almighty God, you prepared a table before me, in the presence of my enemies; you anointed my head with oil and my cup overflows. As a result, your victory, goodness, and mercy shall follow me all the days of my life, and I shall dwell in the house of the Lord God Jehovah, forever. Amen.

(This prayer was inspired on Wednesday, 16/11/2011).

My Inspirations & Appreciation

1. The Divine mission. I was put through an extraordinary life's journey, which I now know was to prepare me for this exercise. One of God's purposes for my life may be to fulfill these literary assignments, leading others to deliverance through the Holy Trinity—God the Father, the Son and the Holy Spirit. All the lessons learned derived from the teachings of the Holy Bible.

2. My late parents Prince & Mrs. J.O. Fasusi (RIP), whom I saw thriving and serving God all their lives in the Church, in their professions, and in their communities; and who raised us their children to know, to worship and to serve God.

3. The teachings of Rev. Fr. J.B Schuyler (RIP), the former Chaplain of the Catholic Church, of the University of Lagos Catholic Community, who counseled me and who gave me a copy of the PIETA Prayer Booklet.

4. My late godmother and mentor, late Mrs. Obafunke Laotan-Fayemi (RIP), a true Mother-in-Israel, who took very special interest in my spiritual well-being.

5. The spiritual support of Rev. Fr. Raphael A. Adebayo, the Parish Priest of St. Agnes' Catholic Church, Maryland, Lagos, who started the program of spiritual support and counseling in the early days.

6. Prophet, Pastor Joel M. Popoola, of the Cherubim & Seraphim Movement Church Worldwide, for his prayerful support.

7. The public teachings of Pastor Gbenga Osho, Prophet & Founder of Laughter Foundation Cathedral, Lagos, and the divine messages he pronounced during church services.

8. The research findings and public teachings of Bishop Matthew Ashimolowo, of the Kingsway International Christian Center KICC. London UK.

9. My daughter, the child from God, Aduraseyi Oluwafunmilola, who became my prayer partner, comfort, support and adviser during the period. She also spent time proof-reading and correcting the draft of the book.

   May God continue to bless and strengthen you all; for those gone to heaven, may they continue to rest in peace! Amen.

REFERENCES

1. "Bibeli Mimo"(The Holy Bible in Yoruba). Edition of 1990. Printed by the International BIBLE Association. P.O Box 225646. Dallas, Texas. 75265, USA.

2. The Holy Bible: KJV. Scripture taken from the New King James Version. Copyright. 1979, 1980, 1082 by Thomas Nelson, Inc. Used by permission. All rights reserved. Printed in the USA.

3. The Holy Bible: Containing the Old and the New Testaments. Old Testament Section. Copyright 1952. New Testament Section, Second Edition, Copyright. 1971. Division of Christian Education of the National Council of the Churches of Christ in the USA. Printed in Great Britain.

4. The PIETA Prayer Booklet. 74th Edition. Published by the Miraculous Lady Of The Roses, 1186 Burlington Drive, Hickory Corners. Michigan. 49060, USA.

5. Grace for the Moment by Dr. Max Lucado. Published by J. Countryman, a division of Thomas Nelson Inc., Nashville, Tennessee 37214. All rights reserved.

6. Freedom from the Grip of Witchcraft by D.K Olukoya (PhD); published by The Battle Cry Christian Ministries, P.O Box 12272, Ikeja. Lagos.

7. Destroying the Works of Witchcraft through Fasting & Prayer, by Ruth Brown. Impact Christian Books, 332 Leffingwell Avenue, Kirkwood, MO 63122.

8. Diagnostic and Statistical Manual of Mental Disorders, fourth edition (DSM-IV), of the National Institute for Mental Health

9. The World Health Organization's Mental Health Atlas 2011, a Research Report.

Printed in the United States
By Bookmasters